Better

Than Prozac!

By Cally Raduenzel

2007
Thank you
so much for
supporting this
wild n' crazy
artist!
you rock!
Cally
Radunzel

Better Than Prozac

By Cally Raduenzel

©Cally Raduenzel 2006

ACKNOWLEDGEMENTS

Special thanks for this book go to:

My beloved family: Barbara (the brains of the operation), Monica, Angela and Melissa Jarrett. My cheerleaders!

The "folks:" Without them I wouldn't be alive!   Kathy Hansen (who believed I could), Richard (Big Daddy and Big Tale teller…I learned it all from him) and Marcel Raduenzel.

Best friends: Jennifer Allen, Jenny C. Adams.

Cousin: Jennifer "Foof" Burman. The family member I'd chose to be my best friend even if we weren't related!

Wish they were here and not in the Hereafter:
My Grandpa Hansen who loved to enchant me with stories

My Grandma Raduenzel who never ever gave up hope.

All these wonderful and amazing human beings have helped me toward accomplishing my life's goal of not leaving this earth without my name in print.

There are many friends and family members who also deserve acknowledgement because I am not an island, and these loved ones have helped me sail through my writer's journey. So, if your last name is Hansen, Raduenzel, Brocke, Burman, or Babbitt, take a bow. You'll be seeing your names sooner or later on bookshelves.

Roommates, co-workers, and lovers I have had, I better give you credit, too, because you have helped to keep me together enough to get to this point.

God bless you, everyone!

CONTENTS

Too Good To Be

True Tales

King of the Boners

When I was growing up, my neighbor Jimmy Zecki was always popping boners. The guy always had an erection, a hard-on, a stiffy, a woody. You get it. I made fun of him and said he was a big loser. He had no facial hair, was skinny, played golf, and when the guys in the neighborhood were bored, they'd dog pile on top of him.

Jimmy, on the other hand, would always tackle my best friend Ginny and me. He'd rub his big ol' boner on our legs, or pretend to bump into us when we were walking home from school. One time when my friends and I were playing chicken in my backyard swimming pool he got on my shoulders and pushed his engorged member into my neck. I heaved him off, and he fell into the diving board. But he didn't care; he just rubbed his head and smiled, trying to hug me.

His dog Doogle was also very horny. Ginny and I figured that he and Doogle were like cellmates who only had each other—love the one you're with or whoever is willing. I'd like to tell you he disgusted me, but instead I was fascinated. After all, I was fifteen years old. When we were in my attic he showed me his prize penis, and it was really big. I gave him a lot of hand jobs. He was a bad kisser, one of those sloppy, vacuum-cleaner-type kissers. It could have been his braces.

One time at Woodmen (ironic) Country Club, Ginny, Jimmy, me, and a bunch of other kids were playing Marco Polo. Georgia McTits (really Georgia Mc Tavish) walked by with her boobs flying free under her bathing suit. She was a lifeguard. Jimmy had the boner of the century, and when he got out of the pool in his scanty swim trunks he displayed a protrusion the size of a king pineapple. All the kids went wild. Jimmy sheepishly grabbed the first beach towel he saw, which ended up being old lady Bishop's coverlet. She screamed when she saw Jimmy's member coming towards her. He took off for the men's changing room and Tommy, the other lifeguard, ran after him. Ten minutes later Tommy returned with Mrs. Bishop's coverlet.

"I had a man to man with him," Tommy said. "The kid's gotta learn to control himself."

Years later, I was at Cy's Pizza with a bunch of kids from my class at college celebrating the end of the semester. I went up to the bar to order another pitcher of Old Style and I heard someone calling my name.

"Kellleee," he kind of sang.

There was Jimmy, wearing a golf cap, swigging a beer.

"What's up?" Oops, I thought, as the words came out. That was a question Jimmy had no problem answering.

He grinned devilishly, "I've been working at the funeral home. What's up with you?" My mind went immediately toxic. Cadavers! Oh, God, those poor dead people.

"I'm just here with some classmates."

"Well, I'm still single." He licked his lips and his eyes shone with lust. Nothing had changed. I cringed, recalling how he used to beg me to "kiss his tree," while he gyrated his hips.

"Actually Kelly, I'm gonna start working at the club pro shop in the spring, so that's pretty cool. Although, the funeral home isn't bad," he said confidently, as if to say Harvard was great, but Yale is better.

"Good for you Jimmy. Well, I gotta get back to the troops. You know how it is."

He patted me on the shoulder and leaned in like he was going to tell me a hot secret. "I still live with my folks so feel free to stop on over."

"Will do," I said, walking away.

When I saw Jimmy's dad at my parents' Christmas party a few years and a ton of martinis later, he kept eyeing me. "Kelly, you look great."

"Thanks, Mr. Zecki."

"Really great! I can't believe some man hasn't scooped you up yet."

"Yeah, crazy," I said, trying to back away.

He followed. "You know Jimmy just got married. He already has two kids."

"I'm not surprised." Yikes. That sure didn't sound good.

Mr. Zecki just nodded with pride. "The apple doesn't fall far from the tree."

"Yes, that's for sure," said my dad, who had just walked up. He didn't realize he was saving me.

They started talking, and I made a hasty retreat. The doorbell rang so I went over to let folks in.

"Well, if it isn't my old friend Kelly," Jimmy said, crushing me with a hug. His wife was a pretty little thing; very timid and well endowed.

The night was long and wearing. I looked around to make an escape. Right before I left, there was Jimmy, scotch in hand, talking to my brother. I bid adieu, but before I could make it out the door, Jimmy straddled me with another hug.

And, yes, he had a boner.

1985

We couldn't drive in 1985. My best friend Rachelle and I lived on our bikes or walked. Our town was smallish but on holidays our folks would take us to Chicago…our city of dreams. Even though it was only forty-five minutes away it seemed like another planet compared to Mohman, Indiana. Mostly when we weren't down the street at The Little Store buying menthol cigarettes or hanging out in Steve's basement watching *Carrie* (again), we were at Rachelle's.

We spent a lot of time in her room or in the bathroom because make-up, hair, and music are what really matters to fifteen-year-olds. We mostly talked about boys, music, and dreams.

"Can I bum a smoke?" I said, sitting on her black-satin-sheeted bed, taking a swig from my can of Diet Pepsi. Caffeine was our drug of choice.

"Yeah, they're next to my jambox." Piles of cassette tapes of our favorite tunes littering her floor and somewhere in her room a guinea pig named Bowie roamed.

We were going through her clothes. I was the fashion consultant since I'd been reading "Vogue," "Seventeen," and "Bazaar" since I was old enough to walk. We laid out all her earrings, bracelets, and make-up on the bed. What to pitch and what to keep? Rachelle was lucky because her mom wasn't a clothes Nazi. She could buy all the cool rock and roll and new wave stuff without getting grounded. My mom did not allow me to dress punk. I could be stylish, but no black, spike-heeled boots, accessories with studs, or too dark make-up. And definitely no big earrings.

"All things with Chinese writing, Egyptian motifs, and neon/day-glow stuff are keepers," I said. Her make up was sparkly and glittered in the dim of her black walls with silver paint splashes. I envied the cool 80's vibe. My room on the other hand was beige.

"Is this cool or what?" She held up a rainbow, unicorn T-shirt in powder blue.

"That would be pitch immediately or burn," I said dramatically rolling my eyes.

"How about these acid-washed jeans?" she said nodding as her spiked Annie Lennox style hair cut glowed with orange cast thanks to our Sun-In spray dye job.

11

Cupping my hand to my chin I assumed a fashion consultant pose and thought deeply.

"Let's cut holes in them; they're cool. Wear them with black and hot pink double-scrunch socks and the black, granny, high-heeled Madonna boots."

"Shirt?" she said, grabbing her latest acquisition out of the closet.

"Hot pink! Awesome!" It read "Express" in black lettering. Its collar was cut off like in *Flashdance*.

"That *is* cute," Rachelle said nodding and putting it on over her day-glow green t-shirt. She was every boys dream: 5'2, big boobs, button nose and a cute baby-face the guys went crazy over. My mom was trying to cheer me up when I said I wasn't cute. Mom explained to me, "Yazmine you are challenging, beauty, and mature…like Katherine Hepburn." It didn't make me feel much better but it did give me hope for when I got older.

Rachelle's mom let her hang posters on her walls which my mom thought was tacky. Oh, how I wanted to hang posters of all my famous loves. Rachelle and I cut pictures out of "Rolling Stone" mostly. Duran Duran, Kajagoogoo, Prince, Boy George, Cyndi Lauper, and David Bowie all gazed down at us like they were our celebrity audience. Some day, I thought, people are going to buy magazines about me —
famous singer and novelist.

We lived in northwest Indiana. Tonight we were going to "Club Soda" in Hammond. "Club Soda" was an under twenty-one club where all the break dancers hung out. It was in a bad area of town but we didn't care. They had video screens! Since no one in our group of friends had cable except for Gina Valasik, the idea of continuous videos was absolutely exciting. That's why today's fashion choices were so important…we had to look cool.

By eight p.m. we were dressed and ready for action! The snow outside was swirling blindly like a hurricane of glittery confetti which only made it more exciting. Our friend, Steve, who was a year older then us and had a red convertible Sunbird, was gonna take us. Neither Rachelle's parents nor mine approved of "Club Soda".

"That place is off limits, Yaz," my mom told me when I begged her to go. "I've heard there are drugs there, and it's in an awful area of town. No way, end of discussion." She shook her blond, streaked, long hair like a Charlie's Angel bursting my bubble of a night at the club.

Rachelle's mom concurred. "If Yazmine's mom says no, then its no."

Earlier that night when we were getting ready to break all the rules we checked ourselves out in Rachelle's moms floor length mirror.

"Does this shirt make me look fat with these pants and belt?" I asked Rachelle as I applied her black eyeliner and gold and pink eye shadow.

"No, I love that shirt."

"Can you believe my aunt bought this for me for Christmas?"

It was a white, almost knee-length shirt with cutouts of old newspaper clippings and neon pink, green, and purple splashes of paint splatter. I put it together with my black leggings and black flats with the wrap-around skinny, loose belt that all the rockers were wearing.

"I love this song," Rachelle said, starting to sing Bananarama's "Venus." The jambox was our other accessory. We took it to the pool, in the car, and to all the house parties. Rachelle and I were great at taping songs off B96 radio. You had to be fast or you'd get commercials or the DJ babbles.

"I made a great mix tape with Depeche Mode, Squeeze, The Police, Go-Go's, and The Bangles," I said.

"Any Boy George?"

"Of course, but you can hear part of an ad for Chess King at the end. I'm also taping Friday night videos so we don't have to miss them, and I told my mom we were going to Steve's to watch a movie and get pizza."

"How much money didja get?" Rachelle said.

"I've been saving. About fifteen bucks. And I've still got twenty from Christmas," I said as I leafed through my purse.

"I also got a bottle of vodka from my dad's liquor cabinet," Rachelle said, with a conspiratorial tone in her voice.

"Perfect. God, Rachelle, tonight is gonna be amazing."

"I hope we meet some guys who look like Duran Duran."

"I want a Nick Rhodes or David Bowie type." I was in Love with David Bowie but Nick Rhodes was my back up fantasy.

"Not me. It's Nick Taylor all the way." Rachelle liked the quiet, dark brooding bad boys.

13

We waited in the kitchen for Steve to arrive. My parents were at the country club and Rachelle's mom was going to meet them there for dinner. Her dad was out of town.

"Girl's, are you sure you don't need a ride?" she said before she left bundled in her black mink.

"No," we both sang out in nervous unison.

We got our coats on and sprayed a little more Aqua Net extra-hold on our hair for good measure.

"Want some?" I said, handing her my bottle of Tea Rose perfume.

"Sure," she said, eyeing my huge, gold lame purse. "Are you bringing that big thing?"

"I have to. It has all my make-up and we're gonna be dancing. I want to look fresh!"

Steve showed up half an hour late and we rushed to his car.

"You shouldn't have been late, Steve," I said. "Our curfew is midnight."

"Yeah, yeah," he said, fixing his hair. The whole car smelled like Polo cologne and hairspray.

We lit up our menthols and took sips of Rachelle's vodka.

"Turn here, Steve," I said.

"I know how to get there," he growled. "Don't forget, I used to live in Hammond. Lisa and Darryl are coming over later. Are you sure you guys don't want to spend the night at my house?"

"Can't," Rachelle said. "Gotta go to my brother's swim meet tomorrow."

When we pulled up, the snow was coming down so hard we almost missed the club. There was a line around the block.

"We're gonna freeze our asses off," I groaned.

We called out the window to some of the kids in line. "How long till they let people in?"

A guy in a Mohawk and a long flak jacket yelled back, "It's packed, so they say every fifteen minutes they'll let another group in."

"Are you guys sure you don't want to come over," Steve asked again.

"No," we both said.

We got out and walked slowly through the snow to the end of the line. My hair was gonna start curling up again and I hand straightened it so great! I even put some pink glitter in it. Suddenly, a paramedic's vehicle pulled up, and a stretcher was brought out.

Everyone inline was muttering about someone O.D.ing. A whole bunch of sweaty-looking people came funneling out, and we managed to get in the club. It was heaven!

It was dark and smelled of body odor, perfume, and cigarette smoke. The place looked so cool. Tables were everywhere, and there were all these little rooms that surrounded the dance floor. One room had a light floor with break-dancers; another had pool tables. There were booths underneath the video screen. I could hear the song "Politics' of Dancing."

"Hurry, let's go dance," I said, dragging Rachelle through throngs of moussed, decked-out teenagers.

We found some guys by the railing that looked older. "Will you watch our coats," I said.

"Sure," said the one who looked like Nick Taylor.

The place was pulsating like a giant heartbeat, and every song they played was great.

"This DJ is the best," I screamed, after song number three— "Erotic City" by Prince.

"We should get something to drink," Rachelle yelled back.

The guys were still there with our stuff, and the one who looked like Nick Taylor brought us two cokes to which we added the vodka.

"You guys don't look very high school," Rachelle said, batting her golden eyelids and letting her shirt slip over her shoulder.

"That's because we're not," one said, shrugging.

"How old are you?" I asked.

The shortest guy, wearing eyeliner and a black, leather jacket with "Z. Cavericci" on it, said, "Doll, we're nineteen."

"Well we're seventeen, so you're not that much older," I lied.

"Seniors?

"Yeah, at Mohman High."

"Snootyville," he said.

"Do we act snooty?" Rachelle said coyly.

"No, you seem pretty cool."

"Who are your favorite bands?" I asked the short one.

"Sisters of Mercy and the Cure."

He had the highest hair I'd ever seen, with long bangs like Robert Smith that covered his chocolate brown eyes. All I could think of was that song "I think I'm in love and my life's lookin up."

"Yaz!" Rachelle screamed. "Let's go to the bathroom."

We slowly made our way to the back of the club. The bathroom mirror was completely taken up with girls shoulder to shoulder, glossing and mascara-ing, spraying and spritzing, while smoking and talking. The heat wasn't on, but with all the bodies it wasn't too bad until you sat on the ice-cube of a toilet seat, which I covered with an inch worth of toilet paper.

"God, my hair looks like shit," I sighed, when I finally got a spot at the mirror.

"You're paranoid," Rachelle said, patting her nose with my Clinique translucent powder.

"No, it shrunk. I look like helmet-head Margaret Thatcher."

"Who?"

"Forget it." Rachelle wasn't into politics.

"What time is it?" Rachelle said.

I checked my Keith Haring Swatch watch. "Dang. it's already eleven."

"Let's get those guys' numbers and do one more dance and then I'll get Steve," Rachelle said.

It was a slow dance to "Sister Christian." When we got back our two guys were waiting for us.

"Phil and Liam went to get the car, but we waited for you guys," the Nick Taylor look-alike said, smiling at Rachelle.

My short guy's name was Sam, and he took my hand and guided me to the dance floor. I could smell his cologne, and his neck was moist and salty, so I kissed it gently.

Sam, on the other hand, took this as a cue to do the vampire's vacuum suction right on my neck and oddly it felt good. I'd always had a thing for vampires.

I could feel a bulge developing in his pants, and it made me feel powerful. But the moment was cut short by Steve screaming at the top of his lungs, "C'mon, let's go." He was waving like a lunatic out of a psych ward and jumping up and down. I could see two bouncers coming up fast behind him.

I yanked Rachelle away from her dude, and we fled off the dance floor just as the security guard grabbed Steve by his shirt.

"Wait! Stop!" I yelled at the Rambo-looking guard with the red bandana. The guy stopped.

"Is this asshole with you?" he said. "He busted in without paying the cover. You've all got to go."

"We are, sir. He's our ride." Being good with authority was my specialty.

Rambo let go of Steve, and we made it to the door. A blast of frigid air hit us.

"I didn't bring my wallet, and there was a cop on my ass," Steve said. When we got in the car, Steve took off like a bat out of hell.

"Slow down," Rachelle and I screamed, as he did a three-sixty in the middle of the street, the car spinning out into a luckily vacant intersection.

"Fuckin' idiot!" Rachelle yelled, smacking him in the head.

"Hey, watch the hair," he whined.

"Yaz, I got Nick's phone number," Rachelle said. Can you believe his name is Nick?"

"Christ. I just realized. I didn't get Sam's."

"He got you, though," Steve said, giggling like a girl. "You've got a hickey the size of Chicago on your neck."

"No! Are you kidding?" I whipped out my compact to see the damage.

"Damn, he got you good," Rachelle said.

"Great! Looks like turtle necks for the next week."

When Steve finally pulled into Rachelle's driveway we sighed with relief.

"Home sweet home," she said, flicking her cig out into the bushes.

Rachelle's mom was up watching *The Big Chill* on video.

"You girls have a good time at Steve's?"

"Great. We watched *Carrie* yet again," Rachelle lied.

"Oh, really? she said. 'Cause I saw Steve at Burger's Grocery buying frozen pizzas. He told me you guys were watching *Sleepaway Camp.*"

"We watched that, too," I said.

She gave us a sly look. "You can sleep in tomorrow. The swim meet's been cancelled due to snow."

"Great," said Rachelle. "Mom, would you take us to the mall?"

"Sure you don't want to go to "Club Soda"?"

Fun In The Sun

I just tracked down my friend Troy in Florida. He said I couldn't have called at a more perfect time.

"Girl, I just got smacked across the face by some white trash." He wasn't even hamming it up in his usual Troy fashion. He was really bummed.

"I move out here for some fun in the sun and three hurricanes hit! I end up living in a rundown trailer park with bad plumbing, my roommate Donna and her elderly parents, across the street from Attila the Baby Maker. It ain't cozy!"

It turns out a little group of kids from across the street has been constantly spying on him while he's on the computer, and to get his attention they throw empty cans on the roof of his trailer. When his roommate Donna goes out to yell at them they tell her to fuck off. This is Troy's cue to appear.

"If you kids don't stop throwing shit on our roof," he growls, "I'm gonna push you in the street in front of a moving car."

The six brothers and sisters run back to Mama who cmerges moments later in her bathrobe and slippers, "What'd you say to my kids, faggot?" Troy repeats the threat, and Mama smacks him so hard, one of her pink Lee Press On's go flying and he has a red handprint on his face.

"So what'd you do?" I said.

"I just turned around, went back inside, and took a goddamn Advil."

"So you're coming back to Chicago?" I said, quietly hoping. "I really miss my buddy."

"Fuck, yes. This place sucks."

60 Seconds Worth of Family Snapshots

How do you deal with an out of control suicidal son and his pill poppin' chardonnay swilling mama?
Send private investigators to keep an eye on them?
Maybe.
Hike up the trust fund till little Jimmy is 60 years old?
Not a bad idea.
BUT...If you're the CEO of a major company you...take out double the amount of life insurance you have on them and rest easy that at least something good can come out of this.
As the old saying goes you can only change your behavior not anyone else's.

Now if a family friend scoffs at AA and says it's a bunch of nonsense she wants other options what might be her remedy?
Electro shock therapy!
Not really the easier softer way but hey, I don't get to call the shots here.
How do I react? "Cause that's really what matters.
Calmly, one must be positive about any form of self help...right?
"Well, Candice I'm glad it worked for you!"
　　　Her tone is more honey than Smirnoff slur. "Ever since my treatment I'm not depressed and I don't want to drink! I gave all the booze to my son!"
　　　"Awesome! I guess that'll give you more time to pursue your painting."
She laughs girlishly, "oh...well...that's the downside. The electro shock zapped that ability right outta my head. BUT I am cooking again...you'll have to come by for some of my Peanut Butter Chicken."
　　　Yea, life's kinda like that.
Case in point. When an ex-Green Beret is bi-polar and doesn't take his med's strange shit can happen. And you can have special conversations like this...
"So Toby's dad shows up with three cases of civil war era ammunition. For Chrissakes its ten o'clock on a fuckin' Monday night and I've got a board meeting in the morning."
　　　"Dude what did you say?"

"What could I say? I mean he's 6'7, and he's sporting a ZZ-Topp beard dressed in full civil war regalia. I just took the shit and put it in the pantry."

"I hope he gets rid of that beard 'cause he's a hottie."
"You better hope no one's watching this guy...shit. I mean Toby's dad isn't even Southern!"

(Side bar: Toby, the Green Beret's son is a gay male model and his lover is a straight arrow banker, with the Harvard version of the Brady Bunch for a family).

Conversations like this prove it's always good to keep in touch with childhood friends...SPICY!!!!!!

Christmas is always a magical family time of year. Too much red wine and gin martini's can alter the warm, fuzzy holiday feeling. Step-mom's can bust the elastic in their 300 dollar silk pants while wielding butter knives at aunts who accuse husbands of sending mother-in-laws to cheap doctors while restaurant patron view the heated debate.

Remedy! Do lunch at TGI Fridays and order the hot cocoa to go!

Two Granddaughters going to Vegas with their retired Metamucil addicted Grandfather can be quite an adventure. But beware of his phone calls home complaining that, "Lacy smoked too many cigarettes and Carlie over spent at the craps tables."
Make lemons into lemonade with one easy purchase! Get three tickets to the cheapest drag show in Vegas and take your ex-football coach Grandfather, his critique of the vacation will surly change.

"It was fantastic! The girls took me to a show and I saw Judy Garland...well, she looked like Judy and when she did Over the Rainbow...I almost cried. They just don't make them like they use to!"

"They sure don't Grandfather!"
"Hey, where's my Per Diem and Anusol?"

To stop this conversation of constipation aids I suggest going for a dip in the pool.
Beware...pool boys in Vegas will think your Grandfather is your Sugar Daddy. Just order a drink and go with it cause they won't believe he's your Gramps.

No holiday is complete without your mom getting smashed and busting a move with your super dorky roommate Kenny.

"Your mom rocks!" He whispered hogging the onion dip as we stood in the kitchen.

"Yea…"

"*I love older women.*" He explained ogling, while leaning on the counter like a three dollar imitation of Humphrey Bogart.

"DO NOT EVEN THINK ABOUT IT! You will never be my step father."

Kenny grins, Snidely Whiplash style, "Don't be so sure my dear."

Warning to all parents! Do not give your pre-teen son the task of giving his elderly great uncle an enema it will result in massive pot smoking and confusion later on in life. Therapy ain't cheap!

Reading this you may think I have issues with my family and friends. INCORRECT! In fact, I just love them all the more. They maybe eccentric but they are NEVER boring!

Swinging Singles

Jerry drove up in his glittery, gold Lincoln Mark V. My mom stepped out of his car in her tight, white hot pants and velvet black halter-top looking very Studio 54. Nonetheless, this was northwest Indiana at 9 a.m. on an overcast Sunday morning.

My step-mom answered the door in her Ralph Lauren, cream cashmere blouse and silk crepe pants. She did not appreciate Mom's nightclub chic.

"She probably spent the night with him," step-mom muttered, wrapping a too large scarf around my five-year-old brother Bo's neck as she crammed him into his sailor's pea coat. Bo started freaking out about her warning not to get dirty. My black, patent-leather shoes were tight, and at eight years old I felt far too mature to have to wear them. Heck, I was already scanning the pages of *Vogue* and *Town & Country* for fashion tips. The last of the melting snow ran like a grey river in the crevices of the driveway as we walked to the car.

"Let's hurry, kids," Mom exclaimed. "It's cold and Jerry's gonna take us to Howard Johnson's for breakfast." She was all smiles in her baby pink, glossed lips and Loni Anderson blonder- than-blond, honey wheat hair, feathered like Farrah Fawcett Major's.

"Hi, kids!" Jerry said in a too loud, faky-nice voice. I didn't like him. He was creepy with his curly, permed Afro, satin polyester, desert-print, formfitting shirt and way too tight leisure suit, imitation jean print pants. He wore a gold chain with a squiggly, dangling charm that looked like a sperm.

My little brother and I got into a huge back seat that felt like an overstuffed couch. My brother looked scared. I could always tell because he looked like he had to either pee or puke. I nodded to him like I would make sure everything was going to be OK.

"Do you kids like disco?" Jerry sounded like Dick Clark talking through an empty toilet-paper roll.

"I like the Bee Gee's," I volunteered.

"Well, alrighty!" He smiled like Jimmy Carter, backing out of our driveway and popping in an eight-track tape. The "Saturday Night Fever" sound track came on with "How Deep Is Your Love."

My mom and him were all kissy, touchy, which I found kind of repulsive. Jerry had pockmarked skin and wore QT bronzer to cover it up. I'd been in his apartment for a few minutes a couple weeks ago. Mom and I were driving to the mall and I had to go to the bathroom. He wasn't home and she gave me the keys so I could run up and go. Alone in his swinging-singles apartment I, of course, had to look in his medicine cabinet: Aqua Velva, half-used tube of Crest toothpaste, Trojan's ribbed ("for extra pleasure") condoms, and some aspirin. There was a box of Tampons under the sink, which I found weird for a single guy. Next to it was a huge bottle of baby oil and a massive jar of petroleum jelly. I opened it and found he must use handfuls of the stuff by the way it was scooped up.

Mom finally came to get me. "What took you so long?"

"Number two."

"I hope you sprayed."

I smiled because I had with his Canoe cologne.

Now we were in his sexy playboy style car. This guy was so "Dance Fever."

When we got to Howard Johnson's it was crowded. But I guess ol' Jerry was a frequent diner because the tiny brunette waitress who giggled endlessly took us to a ripe orange vinyl booth right away.

"I guess you guys don't want the bar," she snickered. Then Miss Giggles set down two adult and two kid menus.

"I'd like an adult menu, please," I said.

"Oh, aren't you just the little lady," she said, patting my blond curls like I was a toy poodle. Jerry spread out like he was sitting in a recliner. You could see his "thing" bulging through his pants. I rolled my eyes and got Bo set up with his complimentary crayons and "Kid's Coloring Fun" menu. Mom light up her Virginia Slim 120 and Jerry lit his Winston. They inhaled in unison.

"Kids, get whatever you want. Breakfast is on me," he said.

Giggles came by with coffee. "Could I get a cup, too?" I asked. "I like it Boston-style, half cream."

"Wow, Cassie, your little girl's got a lot of class," Jerry smirked, pointing his finger at me like a pistol.

"Honey, are you sure? It could stunt your growth," Mom said to me.

"Grandma lets me have it," I whined.

"All right, but just one cup."

Breakfast went smashingly. I ordered the most expensive thing on the menu and Bo colored on Jerry's white, patent-leather shoes. Mom assured him that Fantastic Spray would get the crayon off. When we got back to Jerry's love nest, Mom told us she and Jerry were putting together a bookcase in the bedroom. We plunked down in front of the massive TV console. "Kids help yourselves to whatever's in the fridge," Jer said as they disappeared into the back bedroom.

The place smelled like a musty, cheap motel with the lingering scent of old cigarettes and beer. I flipped on the TV in the living room and pressed the button on the wooden veneer console to UHF so we could get Son of Svengooli's movie pick of the week on "Creature Feature." We sat on faux denim bean bags.

"Now, don't get scared, Bo. It's all fake. These guys are actors."

"OK," he replied meekly. "Why don't you go get us some chips? I'll just stay here."

The kitchen was styled in Early American garage sale. The metal chairs had pictures of the American Revolution that matched the card table. The color scheme was olive, avocado, with burnt orange accents. There were only two glasses in the sink which were filled with yellow slime, so I stood on a chair and pulled a couple of coffee mugs from the cupboard. One said, "Foxy Lady," and the other was from State Farm Insurance. It read "Like a Good Neighbor State Farm Is There."

The refrigerator was pretty sad, too; it held an onion, some coffee, a bottle of club soda, and some yellow mustard.

"Yuck!"

I checked the rest of the cupboards and found some Tang and an open box of Wheatsworth crackers.

"This is all I found," I said, handing my brother the Foxy Lady mug with Tang in it. "Two hands," I reminded him. He was only five.

"Will I get dirty from this floor?"

"No… I think it's OK."

Telly Savalas was starring in *Terror Train*.

"Caggy, this movie scares me," Bo said.

He couldn't say Cassie yet, so his name for me was Caggy.

"Bo, you've watched Kojak with Dad, you know, the policeman with the lollypop."

"Yeah!"

"That's the same guy. So, see, it's OK. He'll get the bloody-eyed monster."

"OK!"

An hour after the movie Bo was asleep in a beanbag by the window. I was listening to Jerry's transistor radio. Station WLUP was promoting a rock-and-roll movie called *FM* and Foreigner was singing "You're As Cold As Ice."

I may only have turned nine a few months before, but I could relate to that song. As I looked out the cheap window edged in condensation, a skinny, weak-limbed tree swayed and bent as if it would break in the rainy wind. Everything was gray. I turned back to the wood-paneled, claustrophobic room and stared at the poster on the back of the door. Donna Summer was in short-shorts advertising "Hot Stuff." I thought singles must be the loneliest people in the world next to me.

Props to My Peeps

After seven years of therapy and eight years of AA I have a new appreciation for my folks. Family is quite an amazing thing because for the most part they are in it with you for the long haul. My dad is a business man and an ex-jock he tries so hard to love me even though my life isn't one he would've hand picked in his perfect kid fantasy. I have three step-children and a partner named Jody, she's got a long black mullet and works for the IRS. These are not things he's really cool with but he smiles, takes me to Marshall's for shopping days and bought me a three foot high stuffed animal frog holding a plush red velvet valentine saying "I LOVE YOU." How can you not love a guy like that!

Mom became very religious along the way. She doesn't like the way things are in the modern world. She wants Norman Rockwell but she got Salvador Dali. Yet we hug, eat blue cheese dip and if I have a horrible emergency she has been there with kind words, hot coffee, Gatorade and unlimited amounts of time to talk late into the night.

I have three sets of Aunts and Uncle's. We'll call them #1, #2 and #3 because I love them and prefer not to piss them off. Set #1, are mom's brother and his wife. They are always rock n' roll to me. My uncle is a devout Buddhist with a Dojo, who literally glows with talent (painting and the 12 string guitar) and enlightenment. We use to watch "Kung Fu" together and he's my sensei! His wife's true religion is books. She is the most passionate reader I have ever met. She has worked in libraries and bookstores all her life. Our conversations about books and movies have helped me through many an agitated family gathering. Her intelligence and sense of humor are dinner party salvation for any occasion!

And the most important fact about them both…they laugh at my jokes!

Set #2, My Uncle (dad's bro) is eternally young. Everyone needs a little bit of him in their life. He is all the National Lampoon movies rolled into one. Inappropriate with the dirty jokes and stories, he is full of fun. I don't need to pay for stand up comedians because this guy takes the cake! He is also the champion of all underdogs and a secret Santa who can guess your hearts desire with the blink of an eye. His life would not be complete without my Aunt. She is a military nurse who brings structure to his life and is kind of his patron saint. She reins him in when his underwear washing adventures get too colorful. You'll never be bored with these two world travelers. They taught me to work hard and live well because life is for the living…don't miss a thing kid!

Set #3, Ozzie and Harriet of Indiana catholic style! They are the Brooks Brothers, Martha Stewart, PTA and bible study conservatives. Polite, hard working, thank-you note writings, matching towels-midnight curfew types whose strength and kindness gave me some of the fondest memories of my childhood. There is nothing more sublime than a morning breakfast with all my cousins and my aunt and uncle over a Christmas weekend at their house. When my step mom had cancer I spent the summer with them and it was a safe place to soothe my fears…and hope for miracles.

I cannot forget to include one of THEE most pivotal forces in my life…my step mom. She kind of hates me but I've learned to have a new appreciation of her. She was there! What I mean is she raised me day in and day out from the age of 5 to 18 (I lived with my dad and step mom). She got me tutors to help me with my dyslexia, math and reading problems. She took me to the doctors and made sure I had good health care. She read to my brother and me in her big cozy bed when we were little and taught me my love of reading. She gave me a taste of the finer things in life like theatre, beautiful clothes and jewelry and traveling. She also taught me the importance of education. We always had a great time shopping and getting facials. She does buy the best Christmas presents and no one can stuff a stocking like her!

I don't want to leave out my brother although I am sure he would prefer it!
He's one of the few people who continually crack me up to the point of belly-laugh-tears. He is the person who centers me. Why? Your guess is as good as mine. We only talk about five times a year but there is an unspoken bond that transcends any thing explainable. I guess that's sib's for you!

None of us are saints and we've all had our arguments but the bottom line is if you can get over the "I'm a victim of my childhood" shit, you can move on and see that it wasn't all bad in fact it was a hell of a ride and continues to be.

God Bless My Family!

Around the

Campfire

Ageless

When I was a boy I would stare at Miss Claire all the time. She was beautiful in a far-off, distracted, long-lost way. The kind of woman you only see in old photographs or in paintings in museums. I remember her because she was my first love. She was a hairdresser in the shop my mom went to and she, honest to God, was the nicest lady I ever met. She had this gift for giving people what they always wanted or had secretly dreamed of feeling. It was like she could read your soul.

The first time I met her I was about ten years old, a total nerd outcast. My hair was in a bowl cut, I talked too fast, and because of an injury, I walked with a cane. She knew instinctively I liked comics and video games. Maybe not such a far stretch if you're a shut-in.

"Is that your light saber?" she winked when I tried to hide the old-man's wooden cane mom had bought for me. Before I could answer she told me about a car accident she'd been in where she'd broken her neck. "It was a miracle that I'm not a quadriplegic," she said, parting my hair off to the side with her pink comb. Her blue-green eyes blinked beneath lightly darkened lashes; her glossy, rosebud lips smiled. Miss Claire's skin seemed to reflect the light, like one minute you saw her and the next you wondered if she was just a dream.

I rambled on a mile a minute about this video game I'd created and she listened like I was the most interesting person she'd ever met. When she washed my hair after using the clippers, well, let's just say I felt more like a man then a boy. The way she spoke in this low voice just soothed all the insecurity and awkwardness right out of me. I was enchanted.

She finished the haircut and exclaimed, "There you go, and you look just like Keanu Reeves!"

"Miss Claire, how did you know, he's my favorite actor?" I gushed, blushing and hopping out of her barber chair.

After mom paid for our haircuts, Miss Claire walked us to the door. She gave my mom one of those two-handed shakes my mom just loves, and then she was off, welcoming some poor chap in a wheelchair.

"Wow," I heard her say before the door chimed closed, "that must be the Cadillac of wheelchairs. What kinda mileage ya get on that thing?"

When I looked back for one last peek through the beauty shop window, you should have seen the look on the guy's face...tickled pink! To Miss Claire everyone was beautiful, amazing, interesting, and lovable.

Skipping ahead to my eighteenth birthday, I was no longer the awkward, pimpled stump of a boy I once was. My gal Linda and I were having dinner, celebrating our high school graduation. The place was dimly light, had cozy leather booths, and was packed to the gills. I went to the bar where I knew Abe the bartender would serve us two glasses of sparkling wine to celebrate. I sat on a leather-backed stool while old Abe poured, his thick, furrowed brow bent to the business at hand. I made a little conversation as he rang me up.

"Thought I just saw Miss Claire walk out of here," he said. "She's so pretty I just can't believe she's not married. A raven-haired beauty like her should be on the silver screen. Reminds me of Catherine Zeta-Jones." Abe set the two full glasses of bubbly in front of me.

I squinted because I was sure I didn't hear him right. "You mean Miss Claire from the beauty shop?" I said.

He chuckled and gave me a queer look. "The one and only. So pleasant, yet fiery. Yep, she woulda made a great star!"

Maybe Abe had imbibed one too many of his own concoctions because for as long as I can recall Miss Claire's had always been a curly platinum-blond. When I got back to the table I told Linda about poor old senile Abe, and she laughed like I was the crazy one.

"Sweetheart, I've been going to Miss Claire since I was eight, and she's always had that gorgeous, Irish, red, curly hair. Since I'm one hundred percent Irish you know I'd notice something like that." I started to argue, but then Danny Johnson came up all in a tizzy and started blathering on about his new yellow Corvette, so we forgot about Miss Claire.

The day before graduation I went for a little trim. My hair was prematurely thinning and Miss Claire knew how to keep it trimmed so it looked fuller then it actually was.

"Miss Claire, you're gonna get a real laugh out of this. First, answer me one question. Have you always been blond?"

She laughed in her sparkling-champagne type way.

"Yes, darling, you've been coming to me long enough to know!"

31

I immediately felt relieved. Then I told her the story about Abe and Linda and it was as if time had stopped. The blow-dryers, loud voices, over-head music all switched to mute. She kept talking and somehow we never came back to the subject.

When I handed her a tip, she patted me on the back with a wink. I left and looking back through that beauty shop window it occurred to me that Miss Claire looked exactly the same as she did when I was ten years old. I don't mean she wore her birthdays well. I'm telling you that she had not aged a day since the day I met her. A "Twilight Zone" feeling crept over me. As I went home, I kept seeing images of her face—never a wrinkle, blemish, or puffy eyes. Shaking it off, I ran up my front steps.

"Forget it, you crazy bastard, tomorrow's graduation!"

At the end of the summer Linda and I said our good byes. She was going to State University and I was going halfway across the world to Europe for college. I was in a special program for computer savants. It was going to be hard to leave this little town I loved so much. A place where neighbors looked out for kids and you knew every cop and corner shopkeeper by name. Watching CNN every night I realized how lucky I was to grow up here. The world was a strange and mysterious place to a kid like me.

Linda and I never married each other. She fell in love with a guy from her psychology class and I traveled all over the world these past twenty years making it a smaller place byte by byte through my computer work. But I still read comic books; they travel light.

As I sat in a café in Prague, I heard a woman call my name. Her English was perfect. When I looked up from my espresso, I realized why. It was Miss Claire. I joined her and we chatted until nightfall. She still had not changed, and now she explained why.

"Have you ever seen the movie *It's a Wonderful Life?*

"Who hasn't? It's an American holiday classic."

"Do you recall that first scene where everyone is praying for Jimmy Stewart because he's in trouble? You hear all their little prayers."

"Yeah." I said as I took another sip of my espresso.

She laughed that sparkly laugh that everyone always loved. "I feel so strange telling you now what I've never even said out loud all these years and I do mean many, many years."

Considering I was approaching forty, I had to agree.

"Well, see, I've always loved everything so much, the world, people, animals, every living thing. I get such amazing satisfaction for making things grow and making people happy. I figure all that love is going out and coming back to me, well, somehow it must have had an affect. Then I started to hear peoples prayers…I guess you'd call them that…and I knew that I could be of service…and the aging" she paused and sipped her drink.

"Honestly, I didn't realize it until one day I looked in the mirror when I was sixty and realized I still looked so young." She sighed and smiled kindly. "Yet it was strange. No one had ever said anything to me about it so I didn't pay it much mind. Maybe I thought it was all in my head.

"Then that day when you told me your story something in me saw the startling reality. I began to ask questions of my customers, and they all saw different things in me. Maybe it was what they wanted to see. Maybe I had stepped through a looking glass of perception. I was created and renewed in each one of these people."

"My God, like the fountain of youth!"

"Who knows? I just trust God will tell me when my time's up. I'll get sad or tired, and then. . ." She shrugged her thin shoulders and pressed her pale hands to her cream-silken blouse.

"Until then I'll just go on cutting hair making people feel beautiful or happy or whatever."

Just then our waiter asked if we'd like the check. Miss Claire smiled and touched his hand. He was African-American, a student from London spending a summer in Prague. We had nice chats before.

"Tony, does Miss Claire remind you of anyone?"

"Funny you say that. The moment I saw you," he nodded to Claire, "you reminded me of my mother. She died in a South African hospital giving birth to me. I only saw pictures of her. Like an African princess she was."

He chuckled. "I guess I got my father's looks."

We laughed and she winked at me.

"Guess I'll see you around, Miss Claire," I said.

"You never know."

As she left the café a sweet breeze seemed to follow her.

I've never told another soul about Miss Claire until now. Don't try and find her, gentle reader. You may already know her.

33

Heart Beat City

In an old 80's black and white graffiti jacket Jack walked down a rainy rat infested alley. It was around midnight, he had his headphones on, and the "Police" were singing "Roxanne" - a song about a hooker. There were only a few "ladies of the night" out because of the nasty weather. Finally he saw the glowing light of the all-night convenience store and pushed the door open.

'Pack of smokes and a coffee."

"Eight bucks," the pumpkin head behind the register said, still reading his dirty magazine. The man had that oily, sweaty pockmarked appearance of sloth. He shoved a Twinkie-sticky paw out giving Jack back his change. Jack made his way down the street; only neon bar signs light his way. He'd be on time for his shift at "Babylon", not like the boss cared as long as there was a warm body behind the counter to take money.

Talk about house of sin! The basement was a numbers ring, upstairs, "Private Dancers," and on the main floor each booth either had drugs, porn or magazines and movies to buy. Jack sold pints of cheap booze from behind the counter too.

Jack was as jaded as they come. He'd seen everything and couldn't wait to save enough to get out of this cesspool of a life. The hours suited him (12-5 a.m.) and he didn't have to clean up. An old dude from the nut house up the street did that *lovely job*. Yes, he'd pulled a gun on people before; yes, he'd let the pitbull, chew up a would-be thug. Gunpowder makes dogs crazy and the owner of "Babylon" put it in the dog's food occasionally to make 'em meaner. Sick bastard!

But Jack's options for employment weren't so great. He'd been a roadie, mechanic (till half his hand got sliced off) and a gravedigger. The roadie job was great in the 80's but because an eight-foot speaker had fallen on his face he'd lost that gig and gravedigger was how he'd felt after his hand had gone half missing. Oddly he wasn't a depressed guy; the writing kept him sane. His flat nose the speaker had smashed made him look almost "mafia cool" Doreen had told him before she left to go back to Miami. He couldn't do Miami, too much sun.

The door's bell buzzed and he let in a guy in a white suit (very Tom Wolfe). The guy bought fifty bucks worth of tokens for booth fifteen, Sheila. Sheila played a Stratocaster naked...oh, those crazy art students. Jack settled back in his chair with a comic book and his now lukewarm coffee, lit up a smoke and put his headphones back on. He must've fallen asleep, which was a big no-no and on top of it the cleaning guy was here screaming in his face. "Dead girl, booth fifteen!"

Yup, Jack inspected from a safe distance; she was dead all right. As you can guess he couldn't call the police. "Babylon's" owner Rich was more then pissed and Jack was fired.

Back home he switched on Cartoon Network to get his mind off his bad fortune...and Sheila's. "Shazam" was on; the genie in the bottle thing would be good about now. He changed his clothes and called Doreen. She'd probably be at work by now but it was worth a shot.

"Hi," he said to her sleepy voice.

"Jack!"

"Man, baby...had a bad night at work."

"Come visit me...you've still got the ticket I gave you?"

"Yea."

They talked awhile; he put his cigar box full of money in his backpack and threw in a change of clothes. "Vacation," he smiled. Jack jumped in a cab and directed the driver to take him to the airport. It seemed like he was sitting in the airport forever, waiting for his plane to board. It gave him a lot of time to think. It's funny how your mind always flips into "deep contemplation" when you have nothing to do but wait. Jack finally snapped out of his daze when he heard his boarding pass called.

Jack robotically followed the crowd down the ramp and onto the plane like cattle being headed into a coral. As he passed the first class section, he did a double take. It couldn't be! Were his eyes deceiving him? There sitting smack-dab in first-class was the guy in the white suit that had visited Sheila earlier that evening. He continued to walk down the aisle when he ran into Sheila coming out of the bathroom.

Jack went nuts! How could this be happening? Was tonight all a bad dream? He fell back in his seat. Sheila repressed her smile when she saw the look on Jack's face. She was tempted to just continue to her seat, but changed her mind. She sat next to Jack in an empty seat and patted his leg. Sheila explained that there was no dead girl, just a cadaver they had stolen from the morgue with an added wig and some pig's blood, "looked real, ha...yea one of my reliable tricks stole it

35

from the city morgue" she laughed. "Had some nasty people after me...*you know what I mean...*"

"I got fired because of you!"

"And that's a bad thing?"

He didn't ask for any more details, he'd learned in his life it wasn't a wise idea. The less he knew the better. Doreen met him at the airport and he told her the story. She just smiled. "Well it got cha here didn't it?"

He hugged her...maybe a little sunshine was what he needed.

The Bite

It was the '50s, I was beautiful, and my house was a little Kodachrome vision of clean angles, highball glasses, chrome blenders, and Formica kitchen tabletops. Not that I was a clean freak, but it was expected. I awoke, put on my primrose- pink house robe like I did every morning, sipped my coffee from a china cup, and read the daily headlines. My husband David's pipe smoke still lingered as I sent him on his way with a peck on the cheek and his lunchbox in hand. He had a big day ahead at his nine-to-five insurance office where he some day hoped to have his name on the marquee.

We lived a nice, quiet life with our social schedule made up of the occasional block party or dinner with friends. Hawaiian themes were popular—Tiki torches and pineapple Jell-O molds, which I made from my handy Betty Crocker cookbook. I had been having a little rodent problem because we lived on a cul-de-sac next to a patch of woods. The little mice were non-threatening; their soft furry bodies slinking between the cracks in the floor and into crevices somewhere in the walls. My husband had been setting traps. I was a modern woman I told myself. I will not live in fear of Mickey Mouse!

I began my daily cleaning, when I saw that the mice had eaten a hole through a loaf of pumpkin bread one of the neighbors had brought over the night before for dessert.

"I knew I should have put that into the bread bin," I muttered, disposing of the scattered crumbs and what was left of the loaf. On my way out to the trash bin I had the feeling someone was watching me. I glanced around the backyard. Nothing. So why were the hackles rising on the back of my neck?

I noticed a dead rabbit as I walked slowly out to the trash bin, he lay like an ugly abomination on the perfectly manicured lawn my husband took such pride in. I examined the dead thing. It had a hole in it much like the one in the loaf of bread. I got a gardening shovel and gloves from the shed, dug a hole, and buried the carcass. Again I felt eyes quietly watching me. Thinking about it, I realized it was the same feeling I'd had two years earlier when this rat of a man named Mr. Hopper moved in next door. I turned him in shortly afterward for being a peeping tom. Turned out he was a jailbird who'd once violated a fourteen-year-old girl back in St. Louis. The police found photographs of all the women in the neighborhood in his house. If it hadn't been for me reporting him, he might still be free and acting out his perversions. He sent me a nasty note from the prison upstate saying how he'd get me back. Lucky for me he died in jail.

The day was stunning; a sweet breeze signaled the coming of autumn, and I shivered with anticipation of log-burning fireplaces, down comforters, and brightly colored foliage. I began to whistle and forgot all about my concerns the rest of the day.

"David, would you like an olive in your martini?" I said to my returning husband.

He smiled and lit his pipe as he leaned back in his lounger. "Of course, dear. If it was a cocktail onion, it'd be a Gibson!" We both laughed.

We watched The Ed Sullivan Show and then went to bed. I tossed and turned and restlessly watched the moonlit shadows of trees outside the bedroom window swaying in the wind. The alarm clock ticked like a tapping fingernail. At three a.m. I slipped into my robe and slippers and padded downstairs to warm up some milk. The moonlight was so bright I didn't flip on the kitchen lights.

As the milk began to heat up, I heard a high, painful squeal and saw a brown object sail through the air. It made a moist splat on my linoleum. I threw on the lights and saw a half-eaten, twitching mouse lying on the table. I grabbed a spatula from the hook above the stove, scooped up the mess, and put it into the wastebasket under the sink. When I tried to close the door s something hard blocked it. I tried slamming it and then screamed as half of a claw flew out and began flapping on the floor. I ran to the den, grabbed a large, marble ashtray and clobbered the freakish object. When I got close to examine it, something larger and faster than a rabbit ran by and took a bite out of my heel. I jumped on a chair as blood poured from the wound.

"David!" I shouted, loud enough so the neighbors were roused.

David came storming in. "Sweetheart, what is it?"

"A rat or something bit me. You ought to see what it did to the mouse in the trash!" I was hyperventilating and speaking so fast David could hardly make out what I was saying.

"Come down from the chair. It's OK." He went to the pantry, got a broom, and began opening all the cabinets and poking inside.

"Whatever it was, you scared it away, dear," he said.

"David, this thing was definitely not afraid of me."

"I'll call the exterminator tomorrow."

We went back upstairs and I cleaned my wound in the bathtub. Hope I don't get rabies, I thought, crawling beneath the sheets and tucking them around me tightly. At 6 a.m. I was groggy, but I made David breakfast and kissed him good-bye. Marcia would be by soon for coffee, I felt reassured knowing I wouldn't be alone.

I had just fastened my brassiere when that creepy feeling came back. I quickly stepped into my dress and flats. My wounded heel throbbed. In the bathroom, as I put on my face, I saw something out of the corner of my eye. The thing was dark brown and looked like a long turd. As it scrambled beneath the claw-footed bathtub, I saw that it was also hard and ribbed like the underside of a lobster. It had a number of tiny feet like a centipede, but they were as thick as a chicken's.

I grabbed the toilet brush and stabbed under the tub. I must have connected because the creature squawked something fierce. It took off out of the bathroom. The doorbell rang, but I didn't answer it. I was on a mission. It flew down the stairs. I followed close behind. Just before it shot through the puppy's trap door out of the house, I got a good look at it. Never in my life have I seen such a weird creature. It reminded me of a picture I'd seen in a book about prehistoric things the kind that are segmented with powerful legs and claws...this one was strong enough to leave imprints in my carpeting. And it gave off an awful stench. I figured the chase was over for now, so I quit and let Marcia in. We talked for almost an hour, finishing a pot of coffee and a whole almond Danish coffee cake that I baked.

"Call the exterminator now," Marcia said excitedly. So after she left I rang him up and he came right over! When I told my story to Mr. Lamont from Bugs Be-Gone, showed him my injured foot, and described the creature, he was curious and disbelieving at the same time.

"You say it looked like a lobster-type worm. Am I getting this right?"

"Yes. Maybe it's something from the lake. It looked aquatic."

"Madam, we only deal with rodents and insects, not, uh, fishy things."

I was getting irritated. "If you like, you can speak to my husband." I gave him the phone number of the insurance agency.

"How about I spray and check those traps your husband set?"

"Fine."

Mr. Lamont went out to his car and came back with spray and extra traps.

"Since I really don't know what we're trying to catch," he said, "I'm going to booby trap your whole house. Cover all the bases."

I checked my wallet to make sure I could pay him when I noticed the foul odor again.

"Mr. Lamont!"

Spray tank in hand, he came ambling in.

"Do you smell that?"

He sniffed the air, and then he sniffed some more, squinting his eyes. "I've smelled that before," he said.

He made like a bloodhound, sniffing his way around the room until he came to a curio cabinet I never use. "Whatcha got in here?"

"Dishes, some stemware; I use the cabinet more for storage."

"Store any food?"

"No, for God sakes. This is the living room."

When he pried open the doors we both screamed. There must've been hundreds of dead mice.

"Well, you don't have an insect problem. It must be a larger-type animal. Maybe a raccoon or a possum."

"That's not what I saw!" I yelled.

"Maybe it was just all covered with mud or something."

"I don't care what it is. Just get it out of my house."

When David came home I told him all that had happened. We felt uneasy because we weren't sure we could catch the interloper. Weeks went by without a peep. Mr. Lamont said to keep the traps in place since winter would be coming.

December came with a flurry of holiday parties. I hung garlands and decorated our silver, imitation Christmas tree with blue bulbs. Everyone commented how cosmopolitan I was becoming. Gifts were put under the tree Christmas Eve. I'd found the most beautiful blue tie for David to complement his Brooks Brothers suit. He bought me a new bowling ball for the league the neighborhood ladies had started. And we gave each other the most exciting gift ever—I was pregnant! We were like two kids as we sipped eggnog and David put another log on the fire.

"I just love Christmas Eve," he said.

Around midnight we fell into a deep sleep.

40

A crash awoke both of us. "You stay here," David said. "It could be intruders."

He took his hunting gun from the closet, I pulled the covers up tight, but I couldn't stay in bed. What if he needed my help? I crept downstairs. The living room was dark except for the dying embers of the fire. I picked up one of the long irons we used to stir the fire.

"David," I whispered, "Where are you?"

I heard another loud crash, and the gun went off.

I rushed into the kitchen. David was flailing about, trying to pull something off his chest. He swung around to face me, and I saw the creature burrowing into his chest. I hit it with the poker. It squealed and dropped off. David fell to the floor. I lunged at it, my fear all gone.

"I'll gut you!" I cried, cornering it in front of the back door. We had nailed shut the puppy's exit, and now, in horror, I stood facing the creature. With all the strength I had, I stabbed it. This time I must have hit a soft spot between the segments because green fluid oozed out. The creature screeched like a demon from hell.

I thrust the poker deeper till I had it skewered like a kabob.

David lay groaning on the floor. "There's a trap under the sink, Gloria. Put the thing in there."

Before I did that I wanted to make sure it was dead. I took a carving knife out of the wooden rack and hacked off its head. Its four yellow eyes blinked and its mouthful of sharp teeth hissed at me: "Gloria, "I'll get you yet."

David gasped. "Its voice!"

We looked in shock and horror at each other.

"I know. It sounded like Mr. Hopper."

David got to his feet to look more closely at our dead monster. "You know how Hopper died," said David. "He was locked in a janitor's closet and eaten by rats."

Mr. Soul's Big Moment

As I sat in the plush chair on the studio soundstage, a peaceful twitter settled over me. For the first time in my life I felt like I was right where I was destined to be—at the interview of a life time. I am finally a famous producer. It was a relief forty years in the making.

I have always been an ultimate fan of pop music, movies, and media. The things I felt about certain musicians, actors, and their work have always been the Sanskrit for my life. It wasn't a choice it was just part of me. Probably what kept me alive and out of the nuthouse.

Creative people are always secretly searching for someone in whom they can see their reflection, someone who truly understands their soul. Their work is only part of their soul, a respite from reality, where I believe that for a moment in the music or in the part they're playing they touch God. It never lasts. Each moment is like a beautiful capsule of shed skin, a perfect archival fossil of a moment when they composed their role or song and it is the best of who they are as an entity.

The audience recognizes these moments; that's why these artists are so sought after like the shaman of their time. They fill the void in the emotional psyche of viewers and listeners. Like a drug, these feelings artists produce last with their audiences like a sense memory, a photographic perfume for our lives. Timing has a lot to do with it; our societal mind-set allows an open door, or worst case, a locked box.

Artists, if they are good, grow. "I'm doing the best work of my life," you'll hear them say. Yet artists are not always the best judge of their work while they succeed in their careers. Even if they do know this is "the best" work, people are sometimes unwilling to accept their beloved in a new role. Quentin Crisp put it best, "popularity breeds contempt." Don't over saturate the media or your dog will become rabid...if you get my meaning.

But here I am today! Artists whose work I admired were coming to the stage in a few minutes to talk with me. We are going into the recording studio starting tomorrow. I didn't know if this amazing project would work, but I figured it just might. Every living musician whom I've loved has signed on to work on this album of albums. I would sing and produce, but we would all be collaborators.

I have an ability to mediate and set a stage to get the best out of all these talents. The research has taken a lifetime, but has now paid off.

I was relaxed with confidence. Never before have I felt this way. I knew this would be a musical phenomenon that would be a hallmark in musical history. Here is the irony: I don't read music; I am relatively unknown for my music. Although my voice is my greatest gift from God, it's not what endeared me to these people. It was my writing. As a writer I've got heart and humor, but I am no Capote. Yet, all these artists read and love my work enough to give this a whirl. Cool!

I listen to the first song in my head, Jem, Peter Gabriel, and Pink Floyd together. I hear the base beat from Jem's song "Them," Peter's "Shock The Monkey," and Pink Floyd's guitar solo with Roger Water's lead vocals… my lyrics. It'll appeal to the young because of Jem; the rockers for Floyd; and the art rockers for Peter Gabriel. My lyrics are a cross between Dylan, Nick Drake, and a lyrical Longfellow—visual, soulful, and lasting. Lord knows that in this world, which has become as plastic as a Pepsi commercial, we could use something soothing. I am soothed by the work I do…it calms the animal within…so to speak. No wonder Nick Drake's more popular now than when he was alive. Music soothes the savage beast as even in times of war, emotional famine, and commercial tyranny.

The lights on the stage are finally coming up; I can hear the people filing in. An assistant is swabbing my head and brow. There is a tightening of my wrists and ankles. The other assistant calls time, and I am locked into this moment.

This is it!

I see all their famous faces: Neil Young, Bowie, Jagger, Kate Bush, and Stevie Nicks. So many.

"Now!" A switch is flipped… its electric nirvana!

The faces change. I feel sick and faint as I look to the "stars": Ray Charles, Rick James, Milt Jackson, John Denver, Joey Ramone, Elliott Smith. They seem to wave sadly as I go by. The pain of fame can be unbearable. Jolting! Then I see a new group and my heart sinks. Gacy, Bundy, Dahmer, Speck.

I'm not like them! I can feel my organs begin to fry like an egg on a radiator. I guess I die before I've completed my opus. What a shame; I had so much more to show them.

Channel 5 News at 10 o'clock: "Guard in blue calls time of death. The families of victims of the Rock n' Roll Serial Killer finally

43

find some peace as they shuffle silently out of the viewing room. Time of death is 9:07 p.m., October 13, 2005."

      Coroner's Report (in part): "Tattoo on right shoulder is wreath of thorns with black roses bearing inscription 'All we are is dust in the wind.'

The Kick Inside

For many of us, one of life's goals is not to feel apart from others. We need to fit in somewhere. We search restlessly all throughout our lives wondering where we belong.

Morris Idleberry was given an interesting gift by a strange fellow. It allowed Morris to do what none of us can ever do—be many people in order to find our true place in the world.

* * *

Morris sat in the corner of a padded room; the stale stench of body odor, fear, and germicide made a putrid perfume, which only added to this hangover of a life he'd been given.

"God," he called out, "you have been unfair." He wasn't angry; he was ready to die. He didn't care any longer for his life. He closed his eyes. His body ached, strapped into a urine-stained straitjacket. He coughed and the drugs they'd shot into him began to work their magic. He heard the clanging sound of the security door being opened, and a man in a white tie and tails entered.

"Just come from the opera, Doc?" Morris spat out angrily.

"Don't we look very Hannibal Lecter tonight," the visitor shot back, sitting directly in front of Morris, cross-legged as an Indian chief. Something intrigued Morris about this man. The man's eyes were the color of amber with flecks of ancient, embedded insects to match . . . quite hypnotic.

"You're a sad case Morris Idleberry—no father, mother insane, brother dead, you're an alcoholic/drug addict and you've gone through three wives, one who miscarried. Nobody cares about you any longer. But you never physically harmed anyone, never stole from your loved ones, and you have tried in your messy life to be a decent man. That is rare for a guy like you."

"Doc, I know my story," Morris began to slur. The drugs were kicking in; everything felt fuzzy; he could hear the sound of his own heart thudding. He prayed it would just stop.

"No dice, Morris. You don't get to die today. I'm not a doctor, by the way."

"I need sleep; I'm on tranquilizers."

"Do you want something different for your life, Morris? If you say so now, we can do this." The man sighed and gave Morris a pitying look.

"What'ya think? Sure, I'd like to be different, but I believe I've exhausted my resources."

"I'm going to explain this to you just once," the man said. He looked at his watch, tapped it a couple of times, and suddenly Morris felt completely alert. His mind became sharp and clear; the man somehow gave him a sense of peace.

"So, here's the deal, Mr. Idleberry. You get to be three different people. I choose them; you walk in their shoes . . . literally."

Morris laughed cynically. "Right!"

"Just close your eyes, say 'go,' and you're there."

Morris thought this was one of the stupidest things a shrink had ever laid on him. He'd been through hypnosis, dealt with his inner child, been medicated up the yin yang, and suffered scads of psychotherapy. All it had gotten him was here!

"Fine, doc, I have nothing to lose at this point."

"You have to close your eyes and say 'go.' I'll be keeping tabs on you. When you're ready, you can come back."

"When I'm ready? How will you know?"

"Actually, you'll be the judge of that."

Morris closed his eyes and chuckled, but for some reason a tear ran down his cheek.

"Go!" he exclaimed without enthusiasm.

* * *

"It's not working," Morris said, wrapped like an Indian papoose beneath a pile of covers.

"Son! Git your lazy butt outta bed!" a man's voice shouted. "You wanna stay up all night like you did it's fine by me, but you're gonna go to school."

So this was what having a father was like.

Untangling from the covers, his mouth tasting like curdled milk, Morris made his way to the bathroom. His body was gangly, arms hung loosely by his sides, and his underdeveloped chest would've made Stallone cringe. He'd at least had muscle tone in his old body. He stared wide-eyed at his reflection in the mirror—zits, a scraggly mustache, sunken cheeks.

"I guess I'm a nerd," he muttered. .

He showered, dried off, and put on some clothes he found in his bedroom.

"Wow," he said, looking at the comic art drawings thumb tacked on the walls. "I'm good!" Some of the drawings were of super heroes, but most were of the women of every boy's dream. He heard a scream from below and a thunk like someone had fallen. In a "Keep on Truckin' "T-shirt, he rushed downstairs. The father stood in shock over the mother. Blood poured from her head; she must've been ironing, and the old man must have hit her with the iron.

She was seizing. "Call 911," Morris yelled frantically.

"What! No! I can't. . ." the father whimpered like a three-year-old who'd broken a vase. Morris grabbed the phone and dialed, explaining to the paramedic there had been an accident.

"What have you done, you little bastard?" the father yelled, coming out of his fog.

"What you should've done to save your wife," Morris bellowed back.

"You don't talk to me that way!" The father lunged at him, but the boy was quicker then this beaten-down husk of an old man. "Gonna have two dead bodies for the cops to find," the man shouted as he grabbed a letter opener off the nearby table.

"What's gotten into you. . .*son*," he hissed, swinging his large paw-like hands across the space between them.

"Makin' up for lost time," Morris said in a voice that didn't sound like his own.

The father was red with rage, his eyes bulging like a strangled pug dog. He had slipped into madness.   Morris grabbed a knife off the kitchen table, both men stood in a face off. If the police hadn't broken down the door, one of them, or both, would have been dead. The father went limp and sobbed as the officer cuffed him and took him away.

Morris heaved a cry of real agony as he watched the paramedics try to revive the mother.

"N-o-o-o-o," he wailed falling to his knees as they pronounced her dead. "She was such a good mother," he sobbed. For some reason he felt like he knew her…she was this kid's mother and now he had none, Morris knew that feeling.

* * *

If Sadie hadn't been pregnant, she would've left Bill on their honeymoon. She didn't love him. Bill wasn't a bad guy, but the baby that died two months after the wedding had marked her fate. Sadie loved that unborn baby; she was not ashamed or even dismayed when her folks had demanded she marry Bill or move out. She had always wanted to be a mommy, simple dreams for a simple girl. When the doctor told her she'd never be able to have children again, the baby was not the only thing that died within her. Sadie's dreams disappeared like a desert mirage. The Sadie everyone thought they knew had passed on.

Although she was only twenty-five, she literally transformed overnight into a sixty-year-old woman. Frumpy and dreamless, she was a steward to others. At home, things were spotless as Bill liked. "Babe, can you heat up these mashed potatoes?" he said, seated in his easy chair, placing his beer can on the TV tray, and handing it to her. After the miscarriage, Bill tried to love Sadie, but now, eight years later, they still lived together, but their lives were separate. When she had held the baby in her womb, she never imagined life would turn out this way.

Morris was Sadie. He heated up the tray and brought it back to Bill and watched him take a bite. "Now the steak is overdone," Bill said, handing the tray back. Sadie/Morris padded back to the kitchen. The amber, cut glassware reminded him of Doc's eyes. Sadie's dinner sat cold on the Formica table. He took another TV dinner out of the freezer and proceeded to heat it. He felt the heaviness of her body, bosoms saggy, and arms puffy. A watery reflection greeted him in the sink full of stale dishwater. He looked at himself...it was as if Sadie was inside him and they were now one. Maybe some one had left him for the same reason, he thought looking over at Bill in all his uncaring slovenliness. But now he wanted to leave Bill. Sadie was empty and dying day by day, until only this stranger inhabited her once lively spirit.

Morris put the fresh meal before Bill, and he patted her bottom. "Perfect now," he said. Morris went back to the kitchen, scraped his uneaten meal into the trash, and retired to the sewing room.

"This is no way to live," he heard himself say as he leafed through Sadie's special drawer. Inside were many brochures, but the one he searched for was advertising a cottage for rent in Maine.

"Tomorrow I'll take my first plane flight to a place I've never been," he said through a wide smile.

The next morning, after Bill left for work, Morris cleared the breakfast dishes, did the housecleaning, grabbed his neatly packed suitcase, and checked to see that the plane ticket was in his purse. He didn't leave a note for Bill. Bill would know why he'd gone.

48

"Would you like a beverage, Miss?" the flight attendant asked, wheeling the cart by Morris's seat.

"Yes," he said to the sweet-faced woman. "Coffee."

As the young attendant poured, Morris leaned towards her. "Miss, may I ask you a personal question?"

"I guess," she said, furrowing her brow.

"How old are you?"

She smiled sheepishly, "Twenty-six today."

"Me, too!" Morris said.

"Well, happy birthday to us!"

Morris sipped his coffee, leaned back, and closed his eyes. Sadie had done the right thing by leaving Bill. He hoped Sadie would be happy.

* * *

"Flight 203 is ready to load," the announcement called. Morris awoke in a chair by the flight's gate. His long legs were stiff.   He picked up his laptop and boarded the small, private plane. Its luxuriousness was right out of a movie. A gin martini straight up with anchovy olives was handed to him as he plugged in his computer.

"My favorite," he said to the steward.

"We know," the handsome, uniformed steward replied.

As Morris, he'd been a bourbon-on-the-rocks guy, but the Beefeaters gin was just what the doctor (or this guy) ordered. The walnut-paneled interior was polished to a fine sheen like the violin his mother had given him before she went nuts. Morris's mom had always been fragile, but when his older brother Terry died, she'd gone over the edge.

"Should've let Terry follow his dream. All he ever wanted was to join the circus," she had said that fateful day, smoothing her old cotton dress. "The one place he felt he would've fit in."

Terry was a little person, called a midget by most. His room was homage to all things carnival. He'd created his own Big Top. Photos of Jimmy Armstrong, a famous Barnum & Bailey midget clown smiled from all corners of the tiny space Terry called his room. Terry died of heart complications due to his smallness. Their mother had packed up Terry's room, each piece of memorabilia and all the photos treated like museum artifacts. She'd drink scotch and talk to herself late into the night, reading Terry's personal journals and unmailed fan letters, trying to forgive herself. Before the state took her away, he'd given her back the violin. She'd cast it back at him.

"I had one son. He died," she said, like a child. She had forgotten who Morris was.

The white uniforms took her gently by the arms. "They're taking me to the circus to be with Terry. Isn't that grand," she said to Morris in a manic joyfulness. Those were the last words she had ever spoken to him.

The airplane landed at O'Hare and flash bulbs greeted him in front of the awaiting limo. As the driver pulled away, Morris checked his emails in the computer he found in the back seat. They were all from famous people from what he could gather he was a real mover and shaker. "Guess I'm now an agent," he said.

His reflection on the screen gave back a beautiful Nordic face with the exception of large, long, horse teeth. "I look like Nick Nolte," he said to himself. Everything about Todd Olsen looked large and long to Morris. From what he could gather from the talkative driver, Todd was an entertainment agent representing actors and screenwriters.

The limo snaked through an upscale neighborhood, which Morris instinctively knew wasn't his. The driver stopped, got out, and opened the door for Morris in front of Nathan Small's mansion. Nathan Small was one of Todd's top clients. He was the latest gimmick of reality television—cameras decorated every crevice of his beautiful home. The viewer had an eye into the world of how a tiny person lived, a modern-day Big Top.

Everyone who was anyone ended up at Nathan's. The little guy was a one-man show, singing, dancing, and writing his latest silver screen smash hit for Will Smith and Joe Pesci. Nathan's cameras were turned off today. He'd backed out of his second season of "It's a Small World." Todd stood to lose a nice chunk of change if ol' Nat bowed out, but he didn't relish the thought of confronting his client.

Morris rang the doorbell and a frizzy-haired blond in a running suit answered.

"Thank God you're here. I didn't want to call the cops. He's in the bedroom with a shotgun, and he won't come out. He's been drinking all night." She threw up her hands and stormed away.

Morris knocked on the bedroom door. "That you, Todd?" A whiskey-graveled voice asked.

"Yup. It's me, buddy. Lemme in."

Morris expected an argument, but a series of locks clicked and the door opened. The same chilling sound as the nut house door, he recalled.   The room looked like a circus-style bordello. A red satin spread covered a bed in the center of the room surrounded by antique, oilcloth backdrops of old carnival acts: "The Fat Lady Sings" and "Meet the Half-Man, Half-Alligator.". Nathan was sitting in his King Arthur throne in the corner, a twelve-gauge shotgun between his legs.

"Here's the irony, Todd. I'm too short to pull the trigger with my toe." He laughed hysterically.

"I know what you mean," Morris said.

Nat's face hardened. "How could you know what a four-foot man feels?" His voice dripped with self-loathing.

Morris wanted to explain he was only four feet five inches in his real body. To many little people he was considered almost normal. Terry had been barely three feet six. Their father had left their mother for that very reason. Once dear ol' dad had found out his second son was going to be a freak, too, he had taken off.

Morris had become a writer as an adult because no one needed to see an author to read his books. He had hidden himself away until he began to be published. Then he'd met Simone, his first wife, who had miscarried and left. He could not comfort her. She had been Morris's secretary and a kind woman. Tracy, his second wife, was blind. She had ended up falling in love with another teacher at the school for the blind where she taught.   Martha, his third wife, was also a little person. They'd met in a chat room. He had adored her spicy personality and amazing sense of humor, but by that time, Morris was drinking bourbon and popping amphetamines to meet deadlines. He was a miserable husband. Since Morris was unwilling to seek help, Martha also packed her bags and left.

"Nat, what can I say, man," Morris said. "Life is full of suffering, but if you let it overtake you, the pain wins and you're just a dead corpse. Another statistic on the Grim Reaper's scorecard." Morris's glaring fault as a writer was his propensity to use clichéd phrases. Nathan didn't want to die. He just didn't want to live. Morris understood that feeling.

"Nat, you've achieved what most men only dream of: a successful career and the admiration of your peers. You're not a circus freak; you're a miracle."

51

Nathan laid the weapon down and rubbed his weary eyes. Morris could feel the scales tipping.

"Well hell, Todd, since you put it that way. . ." He laughed, but a tear rode down his cheek.

"You've got a son to live for," Morris said. "Another great reason to eighty-six the gun."

Nathan's face screwed up in shock.

"How'd you know about my kid. No one knows!"

" I'm an agent. I know everything." Morris was glad he'd read the emails from Nathan's wife.

"All right, ya big heathen, get rid of the babe in the other room and call the Betty Ford clinic. Tell 'em to save me a bed, and we got a done deal."

"I think you should call your wife."

"I need to clean that mess up after I clean this mess up." Nathan pointed a thumb at himself.

"OK, got the limo ready. Let's blow this pop stand."

Back in the car Nathan looked hard at Morris. "You're different. Is this the real you?"

"You mean how come I'm nice?"

"Yeah."

"It's me now. Let's just say I'm going through some changes too."

* * *

Morris awoke from his dream. He was back in the nut house, but all his clothes were packed. He was going home. The room still had that awful smell, but he wasn't in a straitjacket. After breakfast he and the male nurse Phillip walked together to the front door.

"Can't believe your leaving, Morris."

"I thought these places were supposed to get you well," Morris said.

Phillip laughed and patted Morris's shoulder, "Hope I never see you again."

"Me too."

So off Morris went, once again among the living. As he crossed Maple and Main, he saw a familiar face, the comic book nerd. He had an Art Institute sweatshirt on. He winked at Morris, calling out, "couldn't have done it without you." When Morris tried to cross the street to greet him, a bus came and took the kid away.

Morris kept walking to the train. A black limo passed by. Todd was inside. He had an interview with Fox News; he smiled to himself when he saw Morris walking down the street. Morris had showed him a window to the world he had never understood, the world of compassion and empathy.

Morris finally arrived back at his little apartment. He took note of the dead fern on the windowsill and a stack of mail on his floor. There was a long red box on his desk, the type usually used for neckties. He opened it and tilted his head towards the warm sunlight streaming through the window. It was a ticket to Maine.

Morris stood erect and tipped his head towards the warm sunlight gleaming through the little garden apartments window.

"I think I shall... *go!*"

The Lamp Post

I had been traveling for days like a gypsy from small, faceless towns to truck stops. After days, I jumped a barge and slept under a tarp. I thought it was dangerous to sleep on a boat, but the tarp that hid me was so thick and held the heat so well that exhaustion overtook me and I drifted off immediately. I didn't know the boat's destination, but to escape my life I needed to erase all sense of time, place, and the familiar. Being as my wallet was essentially bare; I lived as a cockroach might: keep on moving for survival.

Slipping off the rickety, rusted ship was easy; it seemed as if all life had fled the scene after we docked. I waited until the muffled, harsh voices cleared to meet the misty ink of night. There was a scent to the sea air that was slightly foul, stagnant, and more bog-like then an ocean. Ports of call are usually bustling twenty-four hours a day. I figured I could find something cheap to eat and grab a ride with a truck driver, but instead I found a dark maze of closed shops and dusty saloon windows. I scratched my head and kept walking up the cobblestone street. A slick moss seemed to grow and ooze underfoot making my gait slow. I was in no rush, but a cup of hot coffee right then would have been welcomed.

Off in the moonlit distance I noticed tiers of stone dwellings much like those I had seen in the Greek isles of my youth. But these structures built into the hills were dark, as if a great fire had left charcoal soot over the town and blackened it like a Creole fish. It was as if I had been transported back in time for centuries.

As I ambled, I noticed abandoned carts were strewn alongside the road. Suddenly, clouds drifted over the moon and I was caught in a cover of darkness so thick I had to stop, barely able to see my hand in front of my face. I lit a cigarette to comfort the slow-forming hackles on the back of my neck as I saw a dense fog begin to roll towards me. In the midst of the silence, I heard a noise that oddly sounded like sniffing (crazy as that seems).

A lone light glowed to the west. I had a feeling in my chest like the fear of a child making me want to run to the light. But I was a thirty-three- year-old woman, inconspicuous in a stocking cap and flak jacket and wearing old workman's boots. Best to just keep my pace. I tightened the shoulder straps of my backpack and forged on.

A canopy of trees began to arch my way. I had passed from the town onto a remote path, but it seemed the only way to the light, that blessed light. If you have ever walked in a forest alone, you know the further you pierce the interior the cooler and earthier it becomes. My stomach grumbled like a foghorn in the silence, almost embarrassing. The trees tingled with the sound. I was as scared as a kid in a cornfield on Halloween. A sealed crypt-like void of my senses drew sweat to my brow and a quickened pace to my steps.

The stone road gave way to a mushy, gravel mix. Rain must have swept through these parts recently, and as I got closer to the light, a rank, strange smell assaulted my nostrils. I covered my face with the damp muffler around my neck against the disgusting odor. Something on the ground caught my eye. I stooped over to examine it. It was (I kid you not) a red fingernail, the kind you buy in a pharmacy for a one-night event.

My first sign of humanity! I almost laughed out loud, but I was afraid to make a sound. Leaving it, I kept walking, my mouth parched for a glass of water. I began to jog toward the light, still fuzzy in the fog, but growing brighter and less diffused. But as I came closer, my heart sank. I was utterly baffled. The light was a lamp post.

"A lamp post in the middle of a damn forest!" I exclaimed aloud.

The trees shook into a chattered frenzy, as if a wind had rustled their leaves, but there was no wind. I leaned against the lamppost and then fell to my knees. I beat my red, chapped fists against the ground. Wildly, I searched for a house, cottage, shack, anything. There must be someone who put this light here. There must be electricity! I jumped to my feet. I'll follow the wire!

I searched in vain. Nothing. Nothing!

Clearing my head and calming down, I decided to go back to the town. In the morning it would all be clear. I'd find out where I was, get some food, and get the hell out of here. But when I turned around the road was gone. I don't mean it was too dark to see. I mean only forest, leaves, twigs and rock greeted me. The road had entirely disappeared. Perhaps it was exhaustion that made me crazed. I sat by the lamppost and thought back to when I was small. My father used to tell me: "If you're lost, just stay where you are. No need to get lost any further." I took a deep breath, pulled my cap over my eyes, and leaned my pack against the post trying to sleep.

Just as slumber was ready to overtake me, I felt a presence. Forcing one eye open, I saw him, a small, red-eyed child, if you could call him that. He had the look of desperate hunger, starvation almost,

55

more animal then human. This was all so very wrong. I reached into my backpack for a spray can of mace, something no traveler should be without. It was police issue, thanks to dear departed dad who was a cop.

The child crouched like a cat in the shadow; I thought I must be hallucinating. No kid would be out trying to steal from someone in the middle of a . . . then it hit me like a rock. This was a trap, a lure. Weary traveler looks for a light in a dark, strange area. So I did what I hadn't done in 16 years, I prayed. Prayed like hellfire was searing my ass. Prayed for mercy, protection, and help. I looked closer and what I then saw made me gasp. Pairs of glowing, red eyes — the shapes were hazy, but the glow was unmistakable — gathered like wolves ready to eat meat and I knew they meant to eat me.

The child pounced. I threw my arm out to spray him, but he squashed into a wall. As these creatures came closer, they snarled. But they could not penetrate the area lit by the lamp post.   I huddled against myself, not knowing what else to do. I was paralyzed with fear of these wretched, teeth-rotted, filthy-haired creatures. Some went so far as to lick the invisible wall, scratching and clawing, wild-eyed. I closed my eyes and continued to pray out loud until my voice gave out.

Just then a powerful presence of protection curled around me. I passed out. When I awoke my throat was scratchy and my stomach ached with hunger. I was afraid to open my eyes, but I heard birds and felt the sun's rays. Slowly opening one eye, I saw again the gravel trail. I looked for the lamppost. It had vanished. My bones ached, but I got to my feet and ran until I thought my heart would burst through my chest. I heard sounds . . . the sounds of people and industry! The trees parted, my feet hit the cobbled street, and the town appeared. There were no black buildings or horse-drawn carts. I saw sailors and women, businessmen and dogs. I ran into a small shop to purchase a bottle of water. All eyes were on me although I didn't look any different than them. A man took my money and wordlessly glared.

Get to the boat, I said like a mantra. But it would not be as before in the quiet night. Shutters of clapboard windows opened and the sniffing sounds resumed, making me shiver. No one spoke, but the people stopped in their tracks watching me walk to the dock. A man stood aboard the same barge as the night before. He waved for me to come. He asked no questions, but I felt safe. Before he led me to a seat by the railing, he took the water from me and poured it overboard, giving me a flask from his pocket. "Never drink their water," he said. I nodded and drank deeply.

The boat's horn sounded and slowly we set out to sea. As I looked back at the shore, I saw the boy. He was crying, and the tears were as red as the fingernail I'd found on the path on the way to the lamp post.

The Ghetto Of Ghosts

Norton Mc Shale was a real bastard. When little kids saw him coming the hair on the back of their necks would stand up, dog would bark fiercely, and single women would cross the street to avoid him. They all had good reason…he was a killer.

Norton had never been convicted of his most heinous crimes; somehow he'd always gotten away with those. But battery was one of his specialties. Petty theft, rape and assault charges also lined his rap sheet. He'd skipped states like kids play hop scotch and everywhere he went trouble and pain followed.

Today was no different. It was just more or less lethal. "Get the fuck out of my bar," Joe Kimberly an ex-pro wrestler in his mid sixties said with such ferocity the place fell silent. The place was small but filled up with mill workers from the Gas Co plant. No one was in the mood for shit. Lay offs had been bringing grown men to their knees all week.

Norton threw brown bottle of Budweiser at the mirror behind the bar as he made his exit. Joe caught it mid-flight and the crowd cheered as Norton made his exit. Normally the crowd would jump to their feet to kick his ass but no one was drunk enough yet and there was something about this guy that was a little too dangerous.

As Norton made his way to a stolen truck he'd been driving since noon he smirked. "Wait'll you flush your toilet asshole…my little pipe bombs gonna blow yer ass sky high." He didn't know these people…he simply felt like being malicious. He was so out of this bum fuck town. The stupid little armpit of a hell hole with all its sad, over worked schmucks…fuck 'em. No one was gonna tell him where he could and couldn't piss.

Norton began driving. Somewhere around three a.m. he veered off route 41 which was a mistake. "God, what a skid mark of a highway," he said to himself taking another gulp of warm beer. The road got lonelier and the night was so black his head lights barely seemed to guide him. "Screw this…" he pulled his truck over to the shoulder of the road and decided to finish his six pack and take a snooze. He cut the engine and flipped on the boom box he'd found in the back bed, under a dirty wool blanket caked with dry leaves and sand probably from the beach where he stole the car.

"What the hell." He angrily said, turning the dial and not getting anything but static. He'd been listening to it all day. He loved the rap stuff…got his aggression going. Songs about violence and anger…slap the bitches and ho's…this shit was right up his alley.

"Must really be out in the sticks…"

He turned the radio off, finished up his beer and light up a smoke. It glowed extra orange in the dark silent night. A normal person might have been afraid out there in the tar black soundless oblivion of a moonless night…but you have to remember Norton IS the thing people fear not the other way around. One time he was sleeping on the side of the road in some bushes and two guys decided to jump him. The one that got away lost his nose and the use of his penis; the other guy was found in parts under the same bush where Norton had slept.

Norton was smart…or so he thought. If he did damage he was gone faster then you could say lethal dose. He never stuck around. He drove as far as he physically could, stole another car or snuck a ride with an unknowing driver and was gone like fog in the sun. He had never known fear. He had killed his first man at age eight. *His old man* was drunk as a muther fucker, came in to beat him for killing the neighbor's cat but Norton was ready for him. Took a board to the old man's knee caps and let him fall screaming in pain (Daddy-o had bad knee's from doing train repairs).

"Gee, Dad now you're just at tall as me." With that said he took his dads hunting knife, still caked in cat's blood and slit his father's throat. Horror glowed in the man's eyes as he laid bleeding out for quite sometime. Norton ate cookies and washed it down with a Miller High Life while he watched the life drain out of his only living relative. When Daddy-o seemed good and dead he took a bottle of Jack Daniels from under the kitchen sink, poured it all over his father's body, filched the Zippo from his dead father's shirt pocket and set him on fire. He was a devious kid. He had a trail of booze from the father's body all the way to dad's filthy old couch in the living room and the shack of a house went up like dry autumn leaves.

He walked calmly to the backyard, and sat under a swaying hundred year old oak far enough away to get a really good view of the show. He was kind of excited and felt a stirring in his pajama bottoms…and smiled. I am a man now. When the fire department showed up he was all tears. He rocked back and fourth like he'd seen crazy people do in movies. The affect worked great…no one ever suspected a thing.

When they carted him off Mrs. Denfield, the neighbor whose cat Gabriel had been skinned earlier that day, shook her head. She did not feel sympathy. "I wouldn't doubt if that child didn't have something to do with this." Mr. Denfield concurred, "Ma, just close the door and forget about it…none of our business. He ain't our problem no more."

About sunrise Norton opened his sleep caked eyes and licked his dry lips. Rubbing his whiskers, he began to sit up. "FUCK!" He screamed. A woman stood peering in his driver's side window. She held his eyes and he couldn't look away. Her hair was like fire. A red-orange color like last nights cigarette's glowing ash…and so thick and long, pulled back in a clip. He tried to move but he felt a hot, swaying nausea pulling at him. His heart was thudding, beating with a vise like tightness he was sure was a heart attack. A searing, branding iron hot burning consumed his eyes and he wanted to scream but he couldn't! Her eye took him, thunder clouds seem to move across her irises in breakneck speed. Before him flashed every blood thirsty sacrilege to humanity that he had ever carried out. But this time he felt no pleasure from it. Now the pain of their pain, the cries of their voices and the utter terror that was their terror consumed him to the point he passed out.

"Wake up!" A lady guard said gruffly. He backed up in his jail cell like a cornered dog. IT WAS HER! Shaking violently he urinated on himself. Whimpering, he began to cry but the tears felt like razor blades tarring at his eyes. She shouted. "Don't…stop it. You don't get the privilege of tears." And his eyes went dry. She shook her head and the hair seemed to flame around her head.

Norton had seen many dead bodies. Her skin was just that pale; translucent to the point he could almost see the blood pulse through her veins. For the very first time in his miserable life he knew the cold paralyzing grip of fear. It grabbed him as he had so many young scared girls…some just children, and taken their lives like some people toss an apple core out their window.

"Don't you even beg…you had no mercy…why should I."

He mumbled some shit…and she silenced him. His lips felt the ache of a bashed in mouth. He touched them…they felt as if they were sewed shut. His mind raced. Was it drugs…could he have been drugged? "No Norton," she spoke reading his mind. "It's not drugs." She said it now with an annoyed tone to her voice.

"Just sit in your piss for awhile."

With that she walked out of the cell leaving an overwhelming stench of death. He knew the smell from the old lady he buried in the floor. He'd broken into her home, raped her just to hear her scream, then tied her up and made some dinner for himself. He sat at her table, while she watched him eat her food. She wouldn't stop crying so he stabbed her till she shut up and then in a fit of super strength he ripped up her kitchen floor and buried her there. She lived in the middle of nowhere so no one noticed that Norton was there for days. But with no air conditioning and it being summer in Georgia she started to stink. So he hopped in her car and left.

Suddenly he began to cry...he understood how scared and shamed she was and it felt so deeply and profoundly awful he threw up on himself. This cop was voodoo man. She had fucked him up. And he knew he'd never be himself again.

"C'mon, were going to the showers and wash you up." It was the lady cop. She held the cell door open for him. He figured she'd cuff him. She didn't. He followed her down a hall so dark and dank it felt like a root cellar. Finally they came to an even darker concrete room. There was only one shower. He was now alone and the water came out hot and steamy. Norton lathered up with a cake of blue soap by his feet. The bar of soap was scratchy, like the volcanic ash shit his dad use to use to get the railroad grease off his hands. As he began to become clean he realized...another first, that his father was dead. That his dad was the only one who ever gave a shit about him and he'd killed him. He felt the sick sorrow his father felt when he watched his son, watching him die.

Norton balled up under the scalding water and bawled like a baby, rocking back and forth in agony. He'd done this for the police after he killed his dad...but he didn't feel shit then...he was feeling it all now and it was beyond regret.

The water shut off. The iron door opened and a huge black guard stood looking down on him with distain and threw him a towel. The towel was very soft and very white. It smelled of bleach; clean, sanitized and reassuring. The guard motioned for him to walk ahead. He heard from far away a soft voice singing. Warm and hypnotic he followed it realizing he was alone. The guard had disappeared. The song may have had words but he couldn't understand them, all he knew was that he must follow the voice.

61

In a trance he finally stopped. He felt as if he had walked for miles. The song stopped and he felt like a starving man denied food. Norton felt almost insane with deprivation. Loss flooded over him. Every cell in his body beat and pulsed with immeasurable sadness and loss. He was exhausted with emotion and his eyes began to roll up in his head. The black guard appeared, standing over him.

"Ruthie I think he's going into a seizure."

"That's what happens to many people who have been tortured."

Norton knew this woman was torturing him alright; torturing him with the truth of his behavior, his actions…his degenerated life. For a spark of a second he felt lucky…he was alive…and for that second he had a flicker of gratitude. He was being spared from death and he realized he didn't deserve it.

Ruthie smiled. "He's faster then some…depends on how bad they were."

The black man lifted Norton and he stopped seizing but he could not move. He was completely powerless. "Time to make the donuts!" Ruthie, the cop poked him in his side. He was lying on a cot. He had a grey sweat suit on and white Ked's tennis shoes. He tried to ask her what she meant but couldn't speak.

"Norton, you're going to need to do a lot of listening so you can forget about speaking…I know what your gonna say anyway so it's pointless."

He starred at her…the fear took his breath away.

"Your gonna have to know a lot of fear because you've been immune to it for far too long." She scratched her head and sighed. "Now you're going to make things right."

She opened an iron door without the aid of her hands or key's. The door just opened and the world became bright and blinding.

"It's not heaven asshole, it's just bright out and your eyes aren't use to it."

They walked down a lovely street that looked like perfect Main Street America. Ice Cream shop, family diner, cobbler shop, hardware store and a gas station all seemed like welcoming friends and it felt so weird. The people who walked by him were not in fear of him. They did not glare or rush away like shooed chickens…the way it had always been. He was just another man, walking down the street. It felt so strange, like the first time he had tried Jell-o. Delicious, but indefinable.

A bunch of men were working on a church. They were rebuilding a damaged portion of the rectory.

"O.K tough stuff, get crakin'...the boys'll tell you what to do." The men were all pretty much like him, rough looking or just odd. That kind of odd that makes you turn around when you're walking past someone on a dark street and you want to make sure they are not following you.

A guy named Nick showed him what to do. They'd been working silently side by side for a few hours when it dawned on Norton he had totally complied with this lady. She'd told him to work and he'd done it. This Nick guy gave him orders and he followed them.

"Weird ain't it." Nick said sanding down a board. "Don't know why you're doing it, you just listen and do what's asked and never even try to run."

"Buddy you don't the half of it," Norton snorted.

The man got a serious look on his face. Then their eyes connected and Norton could see in Nick's eyes the crimes that brought him to this point...to this place. It was as if their eyes were a camera filming the destruction of human life. Norton use to get off on watching violence...not just his own but others. Now it sickened him. He felt a void inside himself but couldn't define it.

"I feel like I don't know who I am." Norton said when they were walking over to lunch. They both took brown paper bags off a table that a little old Granny was handing out.

"Enjoy your lunches boys," she said. And then she winked at Norton and it sent an instant chill up his spine. What was with these people? Was this penance for his debt to society?

"Sort of," Ruthie said answering him from behind. She came out of nowhere.

"Are you God?" He said in his mind without speaking to see if she could hear him.

"Don't play games Mr. and if I was God I'd have struck you down by now...but fortunately for you he's got other plans."

"Plans" was to small of a small word to describe the next few weeks of his life.

He spent all his time at homeless shelters, animal clinics, and retirement homes. He worked as part of a road crew, dock worker, buried the dead, cried with the bereaved, was a crossing guard, and taught kids to swim.

Nick and he were bunk mates since that first day. After about a month he asked him. "Why am I compelled to do this stuff? I mean I actually like it and even when I hate it I can't stop doing it…"Norton laughed uneasily, "I cleaned shit out of a sewer all day Tuesday and I couldn't even complain…I felt grateful."

Nick leaned back on his bunk, "after the shit we've done to this world we are blessed to even clean shit out of a sewer."

"That's how I feel too but I…it's not normal for me."
"You are not you anymore…Ruthie's working on yer soul buddy."

The black guard, who's name was Kim appeared. "You boys screwed up the balance of the universe here," he swirled his fingers in the air. "Now we here are settin' things straight."

The next morning they were finishing up at the church, doing some painting. It occurred to Norton while he was starring up at the cross he couldn't feel anything. He was a zombie. Once in a while some good stuff rolled over him but for the most part he had no urges, no anger, sex urge, joy or pleasure. Even food had no taste and the flowers no scent. The shit in the sewer didn't even bother him. The seasons passed and months went into years. Norton noticed gray hair in the mirror.

"You've done well…you had it in you." Ruthie said poking his shoulder as he raked up the last of the leaves at this disabled guy's house. He had gotten use to her being like a ghost and just showing up unexpectedly.

"Walk with me," she said.

"Some of you men," she said smiling, "and a few women…well I try to give y'all a chance but if they are raw to the bone this doesn't work." She smiled into the sun and he felt the fear of someone weak in the presence of massive power. "Will I go to hell?"

"That's not for me to decide Norton. My job is to right all that you have done wrong if it is at all possible. See God's given me a crack at fixing some of the mess you've created but with death it's final. You murdered innocent people…there is no good deed that is going to wash that away. Dead people don't come back to life. But you re-balanced the tipping scale of violence so you can go back."

"Back?" But before he could ask a question he was back on the highway in his truck. His mouth was still dry and his head hurt. Sunrise. He hopped out of the truck to take a leak and while he was pissing into the bush Nick showed up.

"Nick?" He was ready to say something when he realized Nick didn't know him. In fact Nick slit his throat, grabbed his wallet and took off with his stolen truck. It dawned on Norton that the reason Nick was in that strange town with Ruthie and Kim was to pay penance for Norton's murder.

"Healed two birds with one stone…you both needed to fix your wrongs and you both needed to die," said the ghost of Ruthie, as she towered above Norton's broken body. For while Norton was drowning in a pool of his own blood Nick had just had a car accident and gone through the windshield. Who said there was no such thing as karma!

Way to Blue

I'm sitting in a lighthouse and the wind is rattling the windowpanes something fierce. During the week I work in town cutting hair. I do color and perms. I love it, but my passion is writing. They are the two most constant things in my life.

Four days a week I come out to this place off La Quash Head Point to write my stories. When my folks died I got a pleasant surprise — some money. So I bought this lighthouse from an old guy who still lives here and operates it. He was going to lose this place that had been in his family for years. So I made him an offer:

"How about I buy it and make an office for myself and let you go about your business like you've always done, but now I'll pay the taxes."

"Suits me fine, lady. I don't have no children, so. . ."

So I phoned my attorney to draw up the papers.

The old guy scratched his scraggly beard, lit up his pipe, and went to sit in his boat down by the pier.

When we met for the signing, I gave him a buoy-trap as a gift. He chuckled as we walked the wooden object out to his old Ford pick-up. I had painted a lobster lady on it surrounded by smiling crabs and shrimp with laughing oysters and beady-eyed clams.

"I know you don't believe me, but its good luck," I said as my wild, blond curls "medusaed" around my head. He put the buoy out, and each week it comes up full. He thinks I've got some special magic so he always cooks me something good from the catch. That's our bond. Once in a while we have coffee, too.

My partner Nola and I live in town. She's an accountant. We have a cute, little house, but the lighthouse is where we go to relax. It's where our souls belong. Sometimes I get ideas from the ghosts that live here. They tried to scare me off at first, but I knew they were only nervous thinking I'd take away their special place.

"Guys, I'd really appreciate you not unplugging the coffeepot all the time and blowing out my candles." I said to them.

One day I did get pissed because they crashed my computer hard drive. "OK, you, whatever you are, I'm not here to screw things up for you. I just want to write and enjoy the view. If you take away my stories, I'll sell this place and it'll become a tourist attraction. Then you'll have to contend with a bunch of nosy travelers and their whiny kids."

If anyone would have seen me in those first few months talking to the ghosts, they would've thought I was crazy. Luckily, I was alone, so it was cool. You see, Maine folks don't like outsiders, so I knew the ghosts would hate the idea of tourists more then just little ol' me. This particular batch of ghosts is pretty respectful. They don't read my stuff, or bug me too much, but when they get lonely they want to share their stories, and I honestly love to listen.

Most of them died at sea—surprise! Some of them actually left after they told me their tales. They never came back; maybe they finally made it to heaven. Most of them did bad things when they were living and they feel real bad about it now. Take ol' Captain Charles Wittenhauer. He was the first ghost to tell me his story. It was about midnight and the night was so peaceful his voice shocked me out of the silence.

"This is my anniversary, Miss Bebe."

"Really. Wedding?"

"No. When I passed."

I saw him as dots in the form of a man—like Seurat's pointillism. I tried to touch him, and I got a shock. He apologized.

"I'm sorry," I said. "I just felt bad for you and wanted to pat your shoulder."

"I'd like that, but ya can't touch us." He went on," I was a headstrong man, a real idiot. I was supposed to take the missus and children into town to celebrate Thanksgiving early due to my wife's father being very sick. I decided to check my traps before we left. I had designs on a new skiff to buy, and I needed extra money. A batch from the catch would've helped.

"I also wanted to see a lady. She was going to meet me at my boat."

"Romantic?"

"Ay." I could see the outline of his head nod and hang low.

"So while I'm hurrying to haul the traps in to meet my lady friend, well, I got sloppy, became tangled in the net, and went under. That wouldn't have killed me, I had a knife. But damned if I didn't have a seizure just then and I drown.

"Awful feeling as it's happening. I knew I was going to die. You gasp and fight, but you know. I'd almost drowned many times before. This was different."

"Does the irony escape you?" I said, "getting tangled in your own net?"

He chuckled. "Yeah, I've had a lot of years to play it over in my head. You caught it quick, the moral so to speak. Another irony…when they pulled me out of the drink my nets were full as a pregnant woman about to drop anchor."

He laughed again. "I became the tastiest bait."

I cringed.

"Aw, ya don't feel it. You're already gone."

"Do you know what happened to your wife and kids?"

This time he wasn't laughing. "'Twas awful. Left 'em with my debts, and the lady I'd taken up with she had me a child. My wife felt disgraced. I left a bad legacy."

"Can I do anything?"

At this, he got quiet and sort of vanished for about a week. While I was in town and doing a perm on an elderly lady, I got this really strong feeling like I knew her.

"Miss W, where are you from?"

"Me? Why I'm from here, sweetie. Why do you ask?"

"I don't know. I feel like I know you."

She was dark, and her skin was rough, like she'd spent a lot of time outside. Her hands were like rope knots, hands that had seen hard labor.

"Funny you say that," she said. "When I came in today they said Mr. Charles, my normal hairdresser wasn't available. So I chose you." She smiled, and I could see her eyes were cloudy with cataracts.

She pulled me close. "Don't think I'm a crazy, old, blind lady, but I saw you clear as day. I haven't been able to see anything good since back in 1992!"

"So if I give you a bad perm you won't notice?"

We both laughed. I went back to the lighthouse where Captain Wittenhauer was waiting at my desk.

"I use to have my desk right here, too." He paused, he wanted to say something, and "I see you've met the wife."

"That old woman with the perm?" I knew it the moment he said it.

"Yup," he said.

"I don't mean to be rude, but for some reason I thought you were a lot older."

"Since you can't really see me that's understandable."

"She lives with your oldest daughter," I said.

"I know," he said sadly. "Had my oldest when she was only fifteen years old. I told you I was an idiot. But I did tuck away some money, for when I was gonna leave her and the kids to be with that other woman."

He could feel me tense up. "Yes, it was an awful plan, but I was sick of my life and sick of the kids and I hated this town. I wanted to go to Florida. Could you give the money I hid to her?"

"Sure."

"It's down by the shed," he said, "in a rusty old tackle box. You got to dig it up."

I did so as soon as he disappeared. Nola found me later that day in the shed she had brought lunch for a picnic by the ocean.

"What are you doing down here?" she said.

"Digging up some money that a ghost told me he buried. He wants me to give it to his wife and kids. She's that old, blind, perm lady I told you about."

Nola just stood there staring at me. "Bebe, I think you've been alone up here too long. Maybe we should go for a visit back to Chicago."

"Just chill, I'm almost there," I said, now using my hands. The dirt was getting moist since I was hitting water. "Here it is."

It was an old tackle box like my Gramps used to have.

Nola helped me crack it open. Inside were three bricks of cash wrapped in some kind of wax paper. The money was wet, but not rotten. Nola's face was a mask of utter shock.   We counted the money back in my office, almost four thousand dollars. There were also two gold bands, maybe for him and his lady friend.

"Nola, I can't just hand this stuff to her," I said.

"Could you ask the ghost?"

"I can't just summon him. He just shows up."

"Well, ask him when he comes."

Nola has a way of pointing out the obvious; I'm really bad when it comes to logic. So I waited. I didn't like keeping the money. I just wanted to get rid of it. Finally, around Christmastime the Captain showed up.

"Man, I'm glad you're here," I said. "How do I give your wife the money?"

"She still may have an account at the city bank."

He gave me the account number, and I sent the money and the rings to the bank in care of the account. I sent it instead of bringing it in person to avoid drama because everybody in town knows everybody else. I never saw the Captain again, but I heard through the grapevine at work that Mrs. W had a very Merry Christmas.

The other ghosts got wind of what I'd done for the Captain so I became their vessel for making amends to a world they'd done wrong. It was pretty cool, and their stories got me a contract with a publisher in New York. Nola and I bought a beautiful boat with some of the money. We were out on it sunning ourselves and fishing on a beautiful, enchanted morning in late July.

"I miss the ghosts," I said. "Now that I've run all their errands they don't come and visit."

"But you helped them and now they're at peace," she said.

"Who would've ever thought four years ago when we moved here that this would be our life," I said.

"It's pretty great, and I'm enjoying my first summer of retirement," she said, glowing.

I kissed her with the love that many years together can bring.

"I'm going for a swim," I said, feeling faint from the blazing sun.

Nola didn't swim, but I was a veritable fish. My dad had taught me to swim at the town's pool back in Indiana. When we spent our summers in Michigan I was always in the lake, swimming, sailing, water-skiing, and sometimes life-guarding. One summer, on a dare, I swam across the twenty-two-mile lake. My best friend Jenny followed me in a paddleboat in case I got too tired to make it. But I did, all the way to the O'Connells' pier, and Mrs. O was there waiting to greet me with a jug of water and Noxzema for my sunburn. So I had little fear of water.

But this was not Klington Lake; it was the Atlantic Ocean and I should've known better. I could hear Nola scream when it happened. The current had pulled me far from the boat like a giant hand. As my head was sucked under, I recalled the words of the Captain telling me that you know this time it's different and you're going to die. I stopped fighting; it was pointless. The sun's rays disappeared as I was thrust deeper and deeper. I saw fish larger then our boat, and I figured I was going to be their feast. The terror was gone. I figured I was dead.

Just as I said my last prayer, a rush of water thrust me upwards toward the sun. I came shooting out of the water, almost flying, toward the boat. I could see Nola screaming into the radio. A mile or

70

so away it looked like the Coast Guard was coming. As I reached the boat, Nola pulled me in with her strong arms and half ripped my suit off. She hugged my limp body so hard I thought she would crush my ribs. I coughed up water and vomited over the side. The Coast Guard pulled up, and all the uniformed men just stared at me. One of them finally spoke. "What'dja do? Grab onto a swordfish?"

I passed out and awoke in the hospital.

There were rumors all over town that a strange miracle had happened, and I was at the center of it. People were afraid of me at first. I feared I would lose my job because all my clients canceled on me. But after a few weeks passed, it was all forgotten because I acted like nothing unusual had happened.

Nola and I knew better.

"It was awful," she said at my bedside. When I saw you flying toward me, I was struck dumb. I saw the image of a group of angels carrying your body. They were almost transparent, but they had form. Bebe, you must have been carried five hundred feet.

"The doctors said you must've gone very deep because your lungs had almost collapsed. They couldn't explain it. They looked at me for an explanation. I just told them I was too much in shock to remember anything. But I remembered; I remembered all right."

"The ghosts. I think they saved me."

"I know they did."

Now a Word

From Our

Sponsor

Memorial Day

Memorial Day weekend and everyone is barbequing and full of summer expectation. I worked eight hours at the hair salon making people feel beautiful, hopeful and renewed after a winter of soul-draining grayness and war. War is everywhere and nowhere. It's on TV and in the papers…I listen to NPR and the sorrow sickens me like a passing car accident with white sheeted covered limbs. You know what's underneath but it's too gruesome to truly fixate on. After all I have to go to work, inspire my step kids to want to wake up in the morning and get myself through the day without thinking of my grandpa who just died.

Memorial Day is supposed to be a time to honor soldiers who died in wars defending our freedom. To me it is a reminder that men are dying due to the orders of a president whom I don't trust. But it goes deeper…I've never met a person or known of a person whom I could not see the good in. I can look at the most derelict of people and see a sparkle of something redeeming in them or at least feel pity for them. But our president has got me in a quandary. I hear him and I feel the same way I did when I was a kid and I was being fed a line of bullshit. All the words sounded like they had meaning but really they said nothing at all. Like when I was told she can't control herself that's why she says awful things but she really loves you like her own child. The bottom line was adults kept implying certain adults abused us because they loved us. But then what is love and protection if we are not protected by the ones we are told to trust.

I try not to think too much about the war. For me war is about young men and women dying plain and simple. All the pretty words they use to describe the honor of serving in the war scare me because I know it means hurt. Big hurt. The hurt of parents who will never see their kids again. The world hating the country I love…the country that inspired Norman Rockwell and Currier and Ives to historically illustrate a land I adore for it's hope, hard work and sacrifice for something honorable and noble. The men who fight ARE the brave, honorable and noble but the man who leads them to their death aren't. And all his smoke screens, double talk and spin doctors can't cover that up.

I just want our president to be someone who makes me sleep at night…not one of nightmares of Orwellian proportion. I may not have all the facts but what I know is I am not given enough facts to

74

even call my opinion educated. All I can do is wonder why his people are being fired and fleeing. Why people who work for the CIA are scared of phone tapping and fear losing their jobs. Why did Dick Cheney turn into such a jerk when from what I have read he use to be a stand up guy. Why I am afraid of writing this "story" on my computer for fear of being watched. I'm not paranoid…in fact I realize anything or anyone our president wants to monitor he can and that means me.

See when I was a kid my Grandparents flew the American flag year round. My Grams had special jewelry for the Fourth of July. I learned how to say the pledge of allegiance right along side "Our Father Who Art in Heaven." We went to firework displays and talked about the amazing "Fireside Chats" of FDR, the Declaration of Independence, Thomas Jefferson and his fearlessness in signing his name so that it could be read on the Declaration. Lincoln and how he found a way to bring the north and south together even though it looked like America was doomed to divide.

I would love to know what and who our president is from his own lips not speech writers. I can't even hate him because I don't know who he is…I just know he is a guy who uses a lot of fear and threats to make my mom scared. I know my teenage kids are feeling extremely hopeless about their futures. I know when I see the president on TV I don't want to look at him anymore because he reminds me of those weird grown ups who I never trusted. The kind of "adults" who looked normal but you were afraid to be with alone. I wonder if I sent this piece of writing into a newspaper would I be crucified like newscasters who have lost their jobs, or McCarthy's casualties who lost their jobs and livelihoods back in the day. "Happy Days are here again?" I hope so…I hope underneath our presidents bravado he's a really great guy who is misunderstood…the scary thing is that seems more like a fantasy then me becoming a famous author.

We can't back out of this war now so how are you going to fix this mess Mr. President…how? That's what I'd like to know before it's too late and we become a footnote in history like ancient Greece. At this point all I can do is hope God guides you into a direction that doesn't destroy the land I love and all the things we use to stand for.

Connecting the Dots

Since I was eight I've been fascinated by truckers. It all began when my dad got a CB radio, and my brother and I fought over our "handle." Who would get Porky Pig? Why Porky? Your guess is as good as mine.

We would begin our cross-country family trips each summer from our home in northwest Indiana in our Chevy "Woody" style station wagon, and when we hit the border of a southern state, suddenly it was trucker-radio territory. Some talking was strictly business; some was funny or informative: "You got a Smoky (cop) on yer tail!" And some, to my step-mom's chagrin, was crude. How my brother and I loved the spicy ones. "This ole road sure is lonely. I'd like to find me a mama bear!" The trucker would give us his location, and we'd give him ours, and when we'd pass each other, he would honk and we'd wave.

The CB radio was the 70's version of cell phone/Internet communication before we even dreamed that computers would take over ten years later. My favorite truckers were either gross or horny, or both. The cool thing is they had this code of conduct so that if one of them got too perverted, others would get on his case and tell him to cool it. Most of them had a way of being raunchy without being downright crude. There usually was a "darlin'" they were looking to meet, or a "sweetheart" involved, and some were just happy to be getting home to their families. But I did have the feeling with one conversation that the guy who wanted me to "grease his axle" was looking for more then just rig work. He didn't know I was only eight years old.

It just seemed so natural for them to be sexual beings. There didn't seem to be movies or theater involved or moonlight walks on beaches. The way they fished for love was more like ordering a side of bacon with the eggs over easy.

As I got older, that's what I admired about butch women. Because of their dress and attitude, they just sort of put it out there; you knew their take on things. Later I saw that they could be a little shy at first, but after a few beers, they were pretty straight up (excuse the pun). Since I was like a mini *Frasier* girl, the tough-but-tender chicks were very enticing. I wished I could be that honest and just lay it on the line. You know, be free and open about my opinions and what I was looking for in the love department. In my early twenties I really had no sexual identity, and I admired people who did.

That's probably why I bonded so well with drag queens. Even though I'm very feminine, there's a part of me that's also like a trucker. I also figure that any guy who wants to be or play the role of a gal is OK in my book because it's not easy being a girly-girl. It takes a lot of time, money, energy, and work to look manicured and made up. If a guy is willing to go through all that at the same time knowing that people will give him a hard time, well, he must really want to express his feminine side.

Drag queens take a lot of flak from society; people condemn and ridicule them, just like they do butch women, so it's not a decision to be taken lightly; they have to be very brave. In life, just to be who you are takes a lot of bravery. Most people never break out of trying to please the majority. They take jobs they hate, marry people they don't love, or go to colleges or elect majors they have no passion for in order to fit the mold.

Humor is the great equalizer. I've seen that the healthiest people in the groups I've mentioned above take life very tongue-in-cheek. They don't sweat the bullshit; they don't want to conform because they really can't. Have you ever seen a butch woman in a dress? It doesn't look right. Or a trucker in a three-piece suit? He's practically begging to get out of it. Or a drag queen trying to be tough? He reeks fakeness. These souls are all quick with a joke; their wit and wisdom come from living a courageous life, one that's foreign to many. For me, being who you are and knowing not many will applaud that choice is very brave and should be applauded.

This brings me to Mr. Spock and Data, my two favorites from TV's *Star Trek*. I have adored them from the first time I saw them on the small screen. Their logic has no bigotry because logic isn't emotional. Their neutrality and solidness of character is so grounding in a world fraught with irrationality. Mr. Spock and Data are not violent; they listen and have patience; they judge and make decisions based on the best-case scenario. They're all about mediation and coming to the best conclusion for all parties. These are the people and characters I feel most influenced by. If there were a new "Village People," or super-hero comic book, the Trucker, Butch, Drag Queen, Mr. Spock and Data would be my people.

The list, however, would not be complete without adding the Woman of Color. My self-esteem has never been good. Being around black women who struggle with being mere objects, living hard lives, and suffering with unrealistic ideals of what a woman should be, have taught me that self-love is to be prized, cherished, and protected. They don't walk around saying "I'm dumb," "I'm fat," or "I'm stupid" like I have for years. They taught me not to let any person put you down and not to let magazines and media control how I feel about myself.

Black women taught me to say, "I'm beautiful," I deserve better," and "I'm worth more." They don't let weight, poverty, or bad relationships erase their souls. They fight to maintain their dignity even though our society presents them with so many challenges.

Older black women have certain wisdom, strength, and knowledge of the world that is much like the sages of old, the wise men of the fables. There's this one lady who works at a pharmacy I go to that runs the register on the late shift and who is fearless and funny. I've seen her tell a group of gang bangers in the store to "get on elsewhere!" The amazing thing is they listen and obey. I feel better being in the world with these women in it.

Now all these types of people I've described have variables; generalizing is never a hundred percent, but in my thirty-four years, these are the role models who have helped me to survive and thrive in a world in which I feel very helpless at times. I'll say a prayer of thanks for them tonight.

Flash

Olivia sat in a black leatherette booth next to a rain-splashed window. The few leaves that floated on the tea's surface in her cracked cup tasted and smelled like fragrant dirt as she sipped carefully, while her friend Bradley went back to the Thai buffet for more Pad Thai noodles with peanut sauce. It was raining instead of snowing, which made her a little depressed this close to the Christmas holidays.

A cheap TV sat on the counter about eight feet away. *Entertainment Tonight* or something like it was on. There were so many Hollywood-tell-all shows now it was near impossible to know the difference. It occurred to her how fast and cheap things had become since she was a teenager. It didn't escape her that her 91-year-old grandmother felt the same way. Was she becoming an old curmudgeon?

J-Lo. . .*flash*. . .Brittany. . .*flash*. . .Carmen Diaz. . .*flash*. . .the cast from some forgettable teen soap-opera show. . .*flash*. For thirty minutes these three-second teasers flashed across the screen, and Olivia realized she didn't really care about these people at all. A far departure from her teen years when all she wanted was to be part of that *flash*.

All these images played over and over in her mind like the propaganda films of WWII and certain scenes in *A Clockwork Orange*. She felt that these brain-numbing messages were affecting people byte by byte like the old Indian fear of photographs stealing your soul. America the land she loved was like the Titanic sinking while the band played on.

Olivia's long-held fantasy of becoming rich was slowly being replaced by a search for contentment. Happiness had been redefined for her, no thanks to fashion magazines and nine-dollar movie tickets. A luxury car and a mansion in Miami as benchmarks to fulfillment were no longer the things that made up her dreams. At the same time she felt guilty about letting go of these "Big 80's" fantasies of her teens. Was she wimping out and settling for less?

Bradley returned. "The chicken curry rocks!" he exclaimed, making his obnoxious pig out snorts. The Eddie Bauer-inspired family in the next booth glared at them.

"Do you ever feel bad because you don't want more out of life?" Olivia asked between bites of Spicy Beef and Broccoli.

"What kind of question is that?" he snorted in mid-chew.

Olivia wanted to enjoy the moments of routine that now seemed so desirable, yet the echoes of her parents' big dreams for her nagged like a reaper in the shadows. She wanted success as an artist but chasing the dragon of success was wearing her down. Fame use to represent a door to amazing parties where people mixed from all walks of life talking about politics, discussing humanity, history, art: music was profound and could change culture and save our souls, poetry a snapshot of life through words where most never dared to go; artists were the enlightened elite. Now these people who glossed the covers of "Us", "People" and "Rollingstone" just seemed like advertisements for clothes, cars and perfume.

"Maybe I should quit watching so much TV and reading fucking tabloid magazines at the hair salon," she said.

"Maybe you should start listening to that library of music you have in your basement office," he said.

Olivia used to live for her singing, her writing, and her books. She had over four hundred albums, a bookcase full of cassette tapes, and four CD cases that held two hundred CDs in each. Six huge bookshelves bowed under the weight of her novels, and yet lately she barely listened to a piece of music that wasn't playing in her car. Even then the sound seemed more like background noise. And the books she had devoured late at night sat like corpses in a crypt collecting dust. Nothing seemed sacred or timeless…it had all been sold and warped. Beatles suit ties and car commercials with Nick Drake's music played like worthless elevator music. Pimps who beat and sold women were the men to admire in music. What the fuck?

"Bradley, I think I'm at some kind of weird-ass crossroad in my life. I don't know whether to run, walk, sip my coffee, or even enjoy my morning shit."

"I think you're thinking too much." Maybe he was right. Olivia had studied history. Wasn't this modern age she was living in a variation on a theme? Why did life seem cheaper…maybe because it was moving faster?

By woman's-magazine standards Olivia could never love or be loved without a perfect body, an expensive wardrobe, and the latest beauty products. But ironically, she had great relationships and an incredible wardrobe from The Brown Elephant Resale and Junior League Thrift stores. She had the love of her stepchildren and the admiration of her bosses, co-workers, and peers. And sometimes she knew her parents even admired her.

So what the hell was the problem? Why was she buying the hype?

The more she accomplished, the bigger her goals became, and the more she ran the farther she got from happiness. Expectations were like an anchor overboard. She obsessed about getting her novel published; she was drowning in a sea of media inflicted white noise.

"Don't give up on the music," her brother had said when she handed him a few of her short stories with his Christmas present. Was it a slam?

"I'm thirty-five, too old to go on with my music. All people want to hear is Lindsey Lohan."

"Bullshit. Did you hear the Garden State sound track?"

"Yes, but honey, they don't want another Bette Midler or Barbara Streisand. That's me, not the Jewel or Brittney Spears sound or look."

"Well I'm no reader, but I do listen to music, and I really feel that's what you do best."

Now, her brother was in Hawaii with his wife chasing the Magnum P.I. dream. Because Olivia couldn't travel much due to her small paycheck and lack of financial savvy, she was less than in the eyes of certain family members.

Bradly interrupted her rambling thoughts, "Am I eating alone here…you look positively suicidal…"

"I'm having a 30-something meltdown, Brad. I look in the mirror and I don't know who I am or what I am supposed to be."

"Take it from a fifty year old fag honey…you never will. You need a little faith. Do the right things, listen to the inner voice and quit listening to people who aren't you."

She agreed with Brad. But the committee in her head kept tuning into last weekend with her family.

"How can she visit her brother on a hairdresser's salary?" she overheard her stepmother say over the phone to her grandmother. "How can she throw away her college education from Purdue? She's washing people's dirty heads."

The rain outside had subsided. People were closing their umbrellas and walking a little slower to the bus stop on the corner. A guy in punked out purple hair smiled as he passed. A little kid with a huge back pack stumbled like a turtle trying to walk upright. The TV was still blasting in the front of the restaurant, someone's cell phone kept going off and the little yuppie kid kept starring at Bradly pretending to throw up.

Ad's on the TV flashed Zocor and Viagra and Bob Dylan was in a Victoria Secret's commercial! What the fuck?

Bradly turned to the kid who was pretend puking, "Kid you depress me."

"Everyone in America is depressed it's an epidemic!" She said, as she watched a commercial for Zoloft.

Bradly went for round two at the Thai buffet. Brad had moments of true clarity but then he'd go off into these tirades about killing himself. This was her best friend right now. What did that say about her life!

Bradley slurped some noodles into his mouth and began bitching about the dog he'd just adopted. "Now, that I have this dog I can't kill myself. I've lost my freedom!" he said dramatically for the umpteenth time since they got to the restaurant. She didn't know what to say because when she tried to talk logically to him he got pissed, like he was a foreigner trying to ask directions in a city where they didn't speak his language.

"You're depressed about being depressed and your telling me not to kill myself...oh the irony!" He scoffed and then let out a huge burp.

Since she didn't feel much better than he did, all her advice seemed empty.

"Bradley, you just may be stuck living and have to deal with it."

"And you just may have to deal with not being famous," he retorted, "because that's what your depression is really about."

"I'm not depressed."

"You're in denial. Everyone wants to have your life but you."

That stopped Olivia dead in her mental tracks. She chewed silently on her cold Basil Chicken. She suddenly felt ashamed for her lack of appreciation for all the blessings that she had in her life.

News of the war in Iraq interrupted the regular TV broadcast. Bloody faces, exhausted troops, a President she didn't relate to . . . she thought about how fucking lucky she was. She smiled, thinking about her partner Bimmi and Bimmi's three kids. Her life may be chaotic, but whose isn't. Being a step-mom wasn't all Julia Roberts and Susan Sarandon melodrama. It was harder, but it was also richer.

82

When Bimmi's daughter Tara tried to kill herself by taking poison due to a bullying clique in her high school, that's when Olivia knew she was no longer just the "girlfriend of Bimmi's." Bimmi was working out of town and she had to be the parent. It was stressful and incredibly scary, but when she watched Tara drink that charcoal cocktail in the hospital emergency room and fall asleep, Olivia could only think about how much she loved this girl. She spent ten hours in the waiting room with a sour stomach saying silent prayers: "How can I help this kid? God, I'm powerless."

Tara survived, and after a parade of doctors, therapists, and counseling sessions she was back to her *gothic-teen-angst* self. Not joyous, but normal, as normal as a fifteen-year-old kid could be who felt she hasn't found her place yet. All you can do is hug them, love them, and pray for them.

She made a pact with herself: No more gossipy magazines, or TV shows, and no more comparing her insides to everyone else's outsides.

Olivia gazed at the pink, artificial Christmas tree in the foyer of the restaurant. It was actually beautiful like a pink, frosted cupcake or an over-the-hill fairy princess. Her heart swelled as she rose and pulled on her old, well-loved wool coat, and said in a hushed whisper: "I don't want what you're selling anymore."

*Flash. . .*The Thai guy switched the TV to a game show and Olivia realized she just wanted to go home and listen to Neil Diamond's 1973 album, *Rainbow*. Its original price was $1.19, but to Olivia it was priceless. Maybe she should cut Bradly loose. They were two negative Nancy's and she was actually sick of herself for all this inner bitching. Yea, life wasn't Thrillsville but she would survive this war with herself.

Even Drug Dealers Decorate Christmas Trees

Growing up in Northwest Indiana in the 1980's I didn't know any drug dealer's except the one's who got busted on "Miami Vice" or "Hill Street Blues." Drug dealer's seemed about as real to me as ghosts or sewer alligator's. Yea, they probably existed I just hadn't run across any.

Then I became a student of life and what do you know...I met all kinds of characters including people who sell drugs for a living. Something that freaked me out was that many of them had kids and seemingly normal lives. They didn't live in high-rise apartments surrounded by hot looking super model babes. The ones I knew lived in middle class homes on cul-de-sacs or in mundane apartments or even farms. These people had regular jobs, cavities, needed new cars and clipped coupons.

There's a part of me that feels like an alien coming to earth to observe the Human Condition. Because of my adaptable nature I've been privy to life in every sense of the word yet I always remain a little removed. I've never been a big drug person...yes I've dabbled but the price seemed too high to pay to become too deeply involved...arrests, addiction...ultimately a sloppy, ugly death with no dignity. Drugs are around the music and writing scene so they are just part of life like taxes and talk shows. Also if you're going to be part of artistic life then you'll usually have financial problems which means you'll live in "up in coming neighborhoods" or apartments on the fringe of bad neighborhoods so your gonna know the shady side of life.

I was walking my dog one night right before Christmas. It was late and I was freezing my ass off waiting for Quimby, my bulldog, to drop his last turd so we could go in. There's a house on the corner where people are coming and going at all hours of the night. They have nice cars, they'd shoveled their driveway and they had a beautiful Christmas tree full of white lights that glowed into the darkness. I knew they sold drugs. What kind? Your guess is as good as mine. I'm guessing weed because no one looking cracked out ever came stumbling from their house. If anything they sort of kept to themselves.

I thought of that scene in the movie "Goodfellas" where all these coked up people are trying to make spaghetti. When the normal collides with the abnormal. How our lives are variations on what we think is acceptable and what we think is strange.

When I was going to college I use to drive by the Robert Taylor homes a very rough housing project in Chicago that you can see from the highway. My car broke down and I was waiting for a tow…it was about Christmas time and I saw all these little windows with twinkling red and green lights. Again I was struck by the stereotype of The Projects vs. The Suburbs. Why did I find it so strange to see Christmas in the windows of CHA Housing? Were they not like me? Were they just ghosts…or a TV show…or a far away reality I saw on the 9'o'clock news?

Just then Quimby finally pooped and to my dismay the door to the house with the beautiful Christmas tree opened. I picked up the doggie dropping, saying "hi". The man was taking out his trash, he replied, "Merry Christmas," in a deep kind of quiet voice. "Merry Christmas to you too," I said. We nodded and went our separate ways.

I wondered what he thought of me. He'd seen me using a spatula to scrape the snow off my car (I broke my snow scraper) in a pair of oven mitts (I was missing one of my gloves). Our front lawn looked torn up from animals and teenage kids. We didn't even have a Christmas tree this year. No one was in the mood.

It's funny how we compare ourselves to each other yet in our hearts we all seem a mystery to the way one another really lives.

Vacancy

In the Gothic Cathedral, full of rain weeping webs, oxidized iron latticework, oily dust, old crimson velvet, decayed wormwood, shadowed stained glass and rusty hinges lies something. They are neither sinister nor jolly these collections of souls who wander this seemingly empty womb. Goal-less, endless strings of time-promislessness and dateless, anchored in halls of distant... each year becoming more distant, memories. Lives; lives they didn't appreciate, moments missed, love...real love overlooked...now, pondered endlessly throughout their days.

Nights are forever winter and days always-dusky autumn. For these souls spring and summer are merely snapshots in their memories. This is the price you pay for being unappreciative of the life you were given. There is no hell and fire; just this place. Reel upon reel played over and over in these soul minds. Missed kisses, animals left waiting by the door only food and dish bowls as company, fireplaces never lit, letters left unanswered, lovers dismissed carelessly. Oh, but to feel the warmth of their touch just once more. But instead a phone call was taken, a sports game watched, or resentment held too long. Ballet recitals missed to shop for one more designer dress that now rots in a box in the attic of your lost life. Life is about people...that's what you come to understand too late in this hall of haunts. Too many movies, not enough nature hikes. All that was alive just expecting with anticipation of *your presence*...but you never showed up.

Here the Gothic cathedral is a museum of your memories. A shrine to a life that could have been better enjoyed if you'd spent less time sulking about what you didn't have and instead focused on or even ventured forth to what you had all along. There's a reason cemeteries are full of immense crypts and monuments...it is a desperate reach to be remembered. But if you live a full life, each day like a miracle, a great scene to be treasured, a priceless gift, it won't matter if you have no headstone at all. You can rest in peace, content with the fullness of your life, and not have to wander the halls at the Gothic cathedral.

About the Author

Cally Raduenzel earned her degree from Purdue University and two years later became a hair stylist to support her writing habit. She's lead an extremely eclectic life. Her job career includes bartending at jazz showcase in Chicago, selling futons, waitressing working for two universities in admissions, working for no pay at a record company and even sold wine for two weeks. She was a vocalist for many years with numerous bands who went no where. She really wants you to enjoy this book cause life is too short not to!